Pray Through It

Understanding the power
of sowing and reaping

Remember this:
Whoever sows sparingly will also reap sparingly,
and whoever sows generously will also reap generously.
2 Corinthians 9:6

Rob Morrissette

Big Blue Skies Publishing
Hayden, Idaho 83835 USA

Big Blue Skies Publishing
Hayden, Idaho 83835 USA

Publication/Printing Information

International Standard Book Number (ISBN):
ISBN-13: 978-0-976354-90-1
ISBN-10: 0-9763549-0-X

Library of Congress Control Number: 2005908673

Names and certain details used throughout this book as illustrations have been changed to protect the privacy of the individuals.

Design, layout and published by
Big Blue Skies Publishing
Hayden, Idaho 83835 USA

Cover design and book illustrations by Elizabeth Morrissette, Copyright © 2006.

Printed in the United States of America

Dedication

This book is dedicated to those who aspire to more than just getting by, who are wanting to make a difference in their lives as well as the lives of others, who are willing to do what it takes to see change, and who are desiring to impact the world around them for our Lord Jesus Christ. I also dedicate this book to all those who encouraged me along the way to write it in the first place.

To our Lord Jesus Christ whose boundless and unending love, demonstrated in action, has reaped a harvest in and through us for which we are the benefactors;
To Him who, for those who believe, put to death the reaping of death while making us partakers of life eternal;
To Him who sowed His life on our behalf so that we might live.

For Jesus said,
I tell you the truth, unless a kernel of wheat falls to the ground and dies, it remains only a single seed.
But if it dies, it produces many seeds.
John 12:24

Special Thanks

I want to give a special thanks to my creative,
  wonderful and beloved wife, Liz. . .
who had the vision and ability to see my potential
  when I couldn't see it or lost sight of it. . .
who encouraged me, believed in me and lovingly "prodded" me
  when I needed it. . .
who loved me and hung in there especially during those times
  of my immaturity and bad fruit. . .
and lastly, who I am proud and privileged to have as my wife
  and friend.

There is a special place in heaven for women like her.

Contents

Introduction

 I wrote this book in response to a question I have been frequently asked, usually just after taking someone through a time of ministry. The type of ministry I am referring to involves leading the individual through a process of sharing their present issues, helping them discover the root causes, praying through those issues, and then watching them realize some sort of positive change resultantly. Often they wonder what they can do on their own if other issues come up later. The question often asked is, "Now what were those steps we took when we prayed through things?" And so, here is the answer -- a practical, user-friendly guide to assist in identifying root causes to present issues, and then some guidelines in how to pray through them.

It's very common for us to treat our problems using "surface" solutions and "band-aids", which don't really deal with the deeper issue. Sometimes we are told to just "develop new habit patterns" and "practice new ways of thinking." Don't get me wrong—these can be effective, but not necessarily for all applications. What I've found is that much of the baggage we bring into relationships and new situations has its root in hurts from the past. In such cases, we need to go a little deeper than the typical "band-aid" remedies in order to realize lasting results. Determining whether something is related to a past root cause, identifying that root cause, and then deciding how to deal with it, is what this book is all about.

As you experience for yourself the freedom that comes from applying these principles, you will begin to look at things with a different perspective. I know I did. Although not *all* present problems are related to past issues, in those areas where they are, applying the principles presented in this book has been found to be very helpful.

I have included in the following chapters a number of real-life stories of individuals who have experienced change in their lives through the process of praying through past issues. If you're like me, hearing about what someone else has gone through is tremendously helpful, especially when we can identify with the person in the story. I hope that in reading these stories you will be encouraged and begin to realize there really is hope. Furthermore, I hope you come to realize that our hope is not in the knowledge of our own strength to bring about change, but rather in God, Himself, in what He has done, and in what He is able to do in us, especially as we cooperate with Him.

It has been wonderful over the years to see how the Lord has transformed different areas in so many people's lives as they have prayed through issues from their past. These individuals are often amazed to see how often the dynamics in their interpersonal relationships can change. As a result they start seeing life in a new way. They look at and head into old familiar challenges and trials differently. The circumstances around them seem somehow different, and are seen from a new perspective. The details of life take on new meaning and purpose. For the first time, these individuals are able to understand the "why" behind some of the events in their lives, and things start to "make sense". They feel less like victims of the past and more like a participating, shaping force in their futures. Temptation, though still a struggle, is often not as intense. And, ultimately, by letting the Lord come in and restore them, they draw nearer to God and experience His love, mercy and grace more fully. From this, their stories become a means to teach and help others to experience the same thing. Their lives become a living testimony of what God can do in bringing about change. They learn to minister from the very areas of weakness that once held them fast. And, in growing closer to Jesus their healer, they help others draw near to Him as well.

What makes praying through past issues so powerful is that it deals with the issues lodged in the heart and not just the mind. It deals with the "heart of the matter" from where many of our present day problems originate. Praying through something rooted in the heart, and then experiencing change, truly demonstrates the incredible power that past hurts can have over us. This experience makes real the impact of sowing and reaping in our lives. It also shows us that our response to what happens to us in life affects not only us but those around us as well. Past hurts are very rarely the private issues we perhaps wish them to be. They often become festering sores that touch and infect those around us as well.

God loves us as we are, but He also loves us enough to not leave us that way.

Once Jesus becomes the Lord of our lives, He starts to "clean us up". This on-going process is called "sanctification". Sanctification is God's way of making us more like His Son. He desires for us to be more effective here on Earth, while making us more ready for Heaven. God loves us as we are, but He also loves us enough to not leave us that way. He wants to bring out the best in us—while rooting out the worst in us. What would greatly help is our cooperation in this process. Yet this is something you and I must choose to embrace. Throughout our lives God provides us with opportunities to be shaped and develop. We don't need to worry about how it will happen or when. Our part is just to seek Him and cooperate with the process when it does.

One of the ways I have noticed that the Lord attempts to bring about sanctification in me is by allowing tough circumstances or people into my life that stir-up the very issues that need to be addressed. Perhaps you can relate. When He does this, I have found that He is bringing to my attention those areas that He specifically wishes to heal. Often such experiences are just not fun, nor are they something I would have chosen. Yet, when equipped with an understanding of how to recognize when such incidents are linked to the past, I have discovered that I can embrace these as opportunities for change.

That said, I also need to mention that though receiving healing for past hurts is important, it is not a cure-all or a substitute for developing the character that comes only through patience, perseverance and endurance. It also does not excuse the need to stand strong against temptation, to be self-disciplined, to pray, and to seek the help of others. In addition, unresolved past issues should never be excuses for sinful behavior or thoughts. Further, they are not always the reason behind our present struggles. The hallmark of maturity is taking responsibility for our thoughts, actions and words—no matter what the situation is.

When I was in college I had a professor who was also a professional counselor. He made a statement once that's always stuck with me. When referring to counseling others he said, "I am always trying to work myself out of a job." What impressed me about this was that his goal was not only to help people from his office, but also to teach them how to carry-on the work for themselves when issues would arise in the future.

Though there is no way that you or I can minister to everyone around us or solve all their problems, there is something we can do. One of the ways we can make an impact is by learning about the healing process first-hand and then sharing with others the tools of change that were effective for us. By relating our own experiences and then equipping others with the "tools of the trade", we are able to help them embrace the sanctification process for themselves and then hopefully pass it on to people in their circle of influence. My hope is that through reading this book you will learn about some great tools to further that process in your own life, share them, and then, like ripples in a pond, let them touch the lives of people you otherwise would have never even met.

I have heard it said, "Give a man a fish, and you feed him for a day. Teach a man to fish, and you feed him for a lifetime." May you be fed, but may you also learn to fish and teach others to do the same.

"It's Gone!"

Shawn came in to see me for help in getting over his recent break-up with his girlfriend. Though he loved her very much, there were many times during their relationship when he got angry with her and they fought. With much regret he had come to realize that this was what drove her away as well as some other things. The break-up had also surfaced some other strong negative feelings which he couldn't ignore. No matter how much he tried to reason with himself or share his feelings with those close to him, it didn't seem to make much of a difference. There seemed to be this constant, smoldering rage in his heart, just below the surface.

When Shawn came in for our first session together, he was pretty desperate and just wanted to feel some relief. Shawn had a lot to vent and so I asked him to share freely about what had happened. As he shared more and more about the relationship, he came to realize that whenever he had been hard on his girl ex-girlfriend, it gave her the message that she just "wasn't good enough", although that wasn't his intent. Ironically, this is how he too often felt in their relationship. If he pointed out things he thought she should consider changing, she immediately took it as criticism. This was the source of many of their conflicts.

Added to all this was how their relationship ended. Since she broke up with him so abruptly, there was no closure for him. She didn't want to talk to him or hear anything he had to say. If he called her, she wouldn't answer the phone or return his messages. Consequently, he felt like the bad guy, and that *he* was the one who wasn't good enough. Worse yet, he felt powerless to do anything about it. All of this made him very, very angry.

It is not unlike the Lord, however, to use significant circumstances in life to get our attention.

This was not the first time Shawn had experienced the message about not being good enough. He was actually pretty familiar with such occurrences. However, despite his previous attempts to overcome them, these old familiar feelings would rise up again and again when given the right set of circumstances. You really have to give Shawn credit for continuing on, heading into, and making the best of things despite all this, but these reoccurring experiences had become pretty annoying. They were something he had almost come to expect, but not something he had hoped would show up in his relationship with his ex-girlfriend. It is not unlike the Lord, however, to use significant circumstances in lives to get our attention.

During our week together, Shawn shared about what it was like growing up. He recalled several instances when he felt just like he had in the relationship with his ex-girlfriend.

One such instance was when he was born. Though his mother loves him deeply, at the time of his birth she did not want him. This was something she had told him about but he had never really processed before. During that early period, his mother and father were struggling in their relationship. His mother felt unwanted by his father, as though she were inferior or "not good enough". Shawn evidently had felt her pain, which he then internalized about himself. This early decision set him up to see life through the "filter" of this lie.

Shawn also remembered that while growing up he saw his father keeping promises he had made to others but not to him. This had made him very angry, but he felt that as a kid he couldn't do anything about it. And it was hard to argue against what his father was doing. By keeping the promises he made to others, his father was doing good things, helping people and working hard to provide for his family. But, Shawn still felt devalued since the only promises it seemed his father would *not* keep were the promises made to him. This reinforced the lie he already believed about himself that, "I'm not good enough."

The seeds from negative messages of significant and hurtful experiences got rooted in his heart.

Shawn's father has always been very generous to others and is a very hard worker, providing well for his family. Both of these traits have been a tremendous example for his children. But there were times when Shawn felt that his father and mother would bend over backwards for others while at the same time be too hard on him. This too would make him angry. Worse yet, when he shared his feelings about this they would just react to his anger never hearing what he was trying to say. Out of this experience he further decided that no one would ever give him a break.

These and other experiences began to contribute to and reinforce the way Shawn felt down deep inside. It was as if the seeds from these times of wounding got rooted in his heart and grew and grew, like weeds in a garden.

During this intense time of sharing, I wrote down the details of various hurtful experiences. The ones I chose to focus on were those which had the same negative messages Shawn had been re-experiencing in his adult life. This would especially include those with the theme of "I'm not good enough." Then from time to time we would pause, as Shawn felt ready, so he could be led to pray through these and other such memories. As he prayed through them, sharing what had happened, he took time with the Lord to tell Him exactly how he felt—all the deep feelings of anger, frustration and hurt. This allowed his heart to really feel heard. In the midst of these memories, Shawn had made other negative decisions in his heart as well. These were ones such as "life is harder because I'm a boy", "no one really cares" and "I always have to change."

On the night before our last session together, something very challenging but amazing happened to Shawn. That night he was out late—driving around processing his many thoughts. The next thing he remembered was feeling led by the Lord to drive down a particular street. There he saw his ex-girlfriend's car parked outside someone's house. Without really thinking about it he got out of his car and walked to the downstairs back door, which was open. He decided to check inside and there he discovered that his ex-girlfriend was with another guy.

In the past, Shawn would have been furious and probably would have beaten up the guy. He also would have been very angry at his ex-girlfriend. But, to his own surprise, he was amazed to see how calm he felt. This isn't to say he wasn't deeply hurt by what he had discovered. Yet, in the midst of the situation, he didn't respond like he normally would have in the past. He actually felt compassion for his ex-girlfriend for all she had been through with him. Something had changed within. He had restraint, and the old impulses to lash out weren't there. In addition, this unique situation allowed him to finally have some closure with his ex-girlfriend while at the same time experience the change that had taken place in his heart.

After Shawn left, he drove around trying to process what had just happened. He was stunned and hurt, yet amazed at the peace he felt. Meanwhile, since he had been out so late and hadn't returned home, there was concern that something bad might have happened to him and the police were called. When he did get home, they were there waiting for him.

In the past, whenever Shawn had a run-in with the police, they were harsh and unsympathetic, not cutting him any slack. Often they didn't even want to hear his side of the story. It seemed as if they "had it in for him." You can imagine how this would normally have affected him- - and now add to this the incident he had just gone through earlier that night.

At first, the police were very firm with him about being out so late. But, instead of acting the way Shawn was used to, they asked him a lot of questions and listened to him as he told about the encounter with his ex-girlfriend that night. They were actually supportive, offering advice and affirmation. They assured him that it was okay to feel the way he did. One officer even shared that though he has to be a "tough guy" on the job sometimes when he's at home he cries. They were gracious to him and very sympathetic. For once Shawn didn't feel judged, but rather understood—as if he was finally "good enough" to be listened to and supported.

As a result of praying through some of his past issues, Shawn experienced a new freedom in his heart. An evident change had taken place. This allowed him to be less tempted to react as he normally would have. It was also as if something in him was "gone", something negative which used to tempt people into treating him badly. Days later Shawn shared with me that his inner rage really seemed to have disappeared. In his own words he said, "It's so great-- the anger's no longer there!"

Stuck in a Cycle

Have you ever wondered why certain things keep happening? Have you ever felt like Shawn in the previous chapter—that no matter how hard you try to change or make things better, nothing seems to make a difference? Or maybe you find that in some ways you *have* experienced change, but it didn't seem to last or you got only partial results. Maybe you find yourself getting frustrated, or even angry! Maybe you want give up and say, "What's the use" or "I guess this just must be the way I am." It's like you're stuck--you try, only to fall down again—over and over. The question that you'd like answered is, "How do I break the cycle?"

Maybe you're one of those who *won't* quit, no matter what. Maybe you're one who always resolves to try harder, and apply yourself even more. You're good at developing plans and setting goals. You pray and study God's Word. You read books and go to seminars. You do all the "right" things you know to do. And as a result, in some areas of your life you find success, which is encouraging. Yet in other areas, no matter what you've tried, you just can't seem to conquer the problem once and for all. You find it hard to see *lasting* change. With time, you find yourself falling into the same problematic patterns.

For some of us, these cyclical experiences seem to happen mostly in relationships. With others, they have more to do with circumstances such as finances or work. We may have found ourselves saying things like, "Why do I keep getting involved with men who are...?" or "No matter how hard I try, I can't seem to ..." or "How come whenever _____ happens, then _____ happens?" Does this phenomenon feel familiar? If it does, I encourage you to read on--things in your life may start making a little more sense.

Perhaps you can relate to being stuck in a cycle when it comes to communication. I know I can. It used to be that what started out as an attempt to be heard by my wife would turn into a battle. What started out as a simple discussion, often turned into a "boxing match." Initially I thought my intentions were pure. All I was trying to do was help my wife better understand my point-of-view while gently highlighting the error of her ways. Unfortunately, what resulted was round after round of "husband versus wife"—one knock-down, drag out fight after another! (Or at least it sure it felt like that!)

You see, despite my earnest attempts to share my thoughts constructively, what would inevitably happen is that we would both "lock-down" in defense mode. And then for some reason, whenever we would reach this point, I'd find myself suddenly battling with short term memory loss, and actually forget all those constructive things one ought to do when "discussing sensitive issues with one's spouse." I've noticed that this phenomenon also seems to be conversely connected to a notable increase in one's ability to recall certain "foul" deeds (past punches below the belt) committed by one's spouse. Sad to say, the recollection and sharing of these deeds, as brilliant as it may seem at the time, is never well received, and somehow just doesn't bring about the result one originally is hoping for.

In essence, no one ends up feeling heard. Both parties usually find themselves retreating to their separate corners to lick their wounds for awhile and plan for the next round. Sound familiar? Do you ever step back a few days after a big fight and ask yourself, "What was all that about?" or, "Why do we keep getting into such foolish arguments?"

Well, I'll let you in on something. Although I used to ask myself those same questions I can honestly say now that my wife and I, as a rule, don't fight like that anymore. Back when we did, we were simply ignorant to the fact that there were unresolved past issues affecting us, interfering with our communication style and our relationship. Most of those issues were from times prior to our first meeting. But since coming to understand such things, we've been able to recognize and deal with them. We may not do it perfectly, or one-hundred percent of the time, but at least we've found a tool that truly and lastingly helps.

You may have recently attended a seminar or read some good books on how to communicate with and understand others better. Maybe you have memorized something to help you when in the midst of conflicts, something like "The Six Keys to Effective Communication." You may have even heard how these keys helped countless others. You may actually feel very well equipped to take on whatever comes your way. Maybe you've even felt *excited* to try out

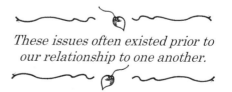

These issues often existed prior to our relationship to one another.

these new techniques on your cranky boss and your silent spouse. And sometimes, lo and behold, you've found that these "Six Keys" actually work! As a result you've experienced some measure of success.

But if, like my wife and I, there have been times when the success doesn't seem to last, or is situational, or you can't remember what you are "supposed" to do, perhaps you might want to consider that there are other things involved – past, unresolved issues.

Don't get me wrong. We'll always have problems to work through, temptations to resist, and circumstances that just require patience and self-discipline. But in some areas of our lives, where there are things that seem to be harder or more discouraging than they should be, we may need to take a closer look, particularly in those areas where we feel overly vulnerable or too sensitive or find that people have way too much power over how we feel.

In some instances, we've become so accustomed to what will occur, we can almost predict it. As a result, we have developed negative expectations as to the way things will "always" go. We find ourselves thinking that perhaps we are cursed or somehow permanently flawed. We begin to think we are different from everyone else—that

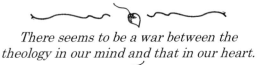

There seems to be a war between the theology in our mind and that in our heart.

others get to be loved, but we don't. In some cases we may even adjust our present theology to reconcile the conflict between what we believe to be true with what we have been experiencing.

In essence, there seems to be a war between the theology in our minds and that in our hearts. We begin to think things like, "perhaps this is just my lot in life, or my cross to bear," or maybe, "joy isn't what I thought it was," or how about, "God has favorites, and I'm not one of them," or "could it be that God doesn't like me?" We often adjust our theology in order to console ourselves, to make sense out of our confusion. Unfortunately, while some people adjust their beliefs to match their experience, others just simply withdraw from God. They might admit that He exists, but they are no longer on speaking terms with Him. They choose a more distant relationship with God over an intimate one.

For many years I struggled in my heart with doubts about God's love for me. I did so despite all I knew to be true about Him. I thought He didn't care. I felt I was on my own to figure things out. I was afraid of Him, not knowing what He really thought of me. God seemed distant and uninvolved. I had been taught that God cared and was always near, that He loved me and wanted a personal relationship, and I wanted it too. Yet, because that was not my experience, I resigned to the belief that a personal relationship with God must not be what I had first thought. Yet one day I discovered that my warped experience was really a by-product of being a child of divorce and growing up in a home where my father was not present. After praying through those hurts I began to see my heart theology change and finally line up with what I had first come to believe about God.

Perhaps you can relate to being overly sensitive to particular people or certain circumstances. I did for many years. Some people just seemed to make me feel insecure about myself, to the point that I became very nervous and self-conscious when around them. As a result, I would avoid them for fear that I would do something stupid or embarrassing. I began to limit my social circle and found I was always calculating my next move, who to avoid, or planning what I'd say or not say, especially in a group setting. All of this was so draining! Sound familiar?

Just think of all the additional energy you and I would have if we didn't have to do all this avoiding and thinking and planning. Yet, when I was finally able to recognize that there were root causes behind these insecurities, and then pray through them, things began to change.

Now there are some people who take life and circumstances head-on, despite all that comes at them, either cleaning-up the

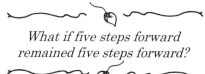

What if five steps forward remained five steps forward?

mess or ignoring it as they go. Their motto is "you might as well take it on, for it sure beats doing nothing!" They push ahead. For every five steps forward they may fall three steps back. But they figure that at least they're making progress. "Besides," they say to themselves, "what else can I do about it?" But why can't they seem to retain *all* the progress they've made? Is there more they could be doing? What if our peace was truly no longer dependent upon our circumstances? What if others no longer had the power to "steal" our sense of self, or redefine who we are? What if five steps forward remained five steps forward? Wouldn't that be wonderful!

There are many of us who have grown pretty weary of lowering our expectations of life. Re-occurring disappointment has brought too much hurt. Within reason, we have presumed that life should be a certain way only to discover that it's not what we thought. As a result, we have found ourselves compromising our goals, settling for less and diminishing our dreams, all in an attempt to minimize the pain of continued disappointment. We find ourselves redefining such things as love, family, marriage and what it means to be a man or a woman. We have altered our view of life to make sense of something we have been unable to fully resolve or explain. Some of us have even given up altogether-- making our experience our truth. Instead of swimming against the current, we've decided to go adrift, and let life take us where it wills.

I used to believe that joy was just a state of mind, a way of thinking not necessarily related to one's feelings. I used to believe that rewards and blessings were things you could experience in the next life but were not to be hoped for while here on earth. I used to believe that anger was a sin despite what Ephesians 4:26 (NASB) says: "Be angry, and yet do not sin." I also used to believe that crying was weakness, that men are not capable of being sensitive, and that all women are controlling. Maybe these thoughts resonate with some of your own personal beliefs. I am happy to say that I have since learned to see these as the lies they truly are and, through prayer, have been set free to redefine them rightly in my heart.

I can imagine that if you have read to this point, you have begun to identify some areas in your life that seem to fit what I have been describing here. This hasn't happened by accident, for I prayed that it would!

The question now is, "what can be done about it?" What is shared in the following chapters is a simple method for uncovering "bitter roots" from the past and then praying through them to release us from the unforgiveness binding us to their harmful influence in the present. This book is meant to provide a basic understanding as to why we often get stuck in frustrating relational patterns and reap unfortunate circumstances. More importantly, it is meant to equip the reader with a biblical means for dealing with them at the root level!

Things to Cultivate

- What type of negative cycles and patterns have you found yourself stuck in?
- What are some of the things you have tried that were helpful in dealing with negative cycles and patterns in your life? Why do you think they were helpful?
- What are some of the things you have tried that have not been so helpful in dealing with negative cycles and patterns in your life? Why do think they were not helpful?
- In what areas have you found yourself lowering your expectations because of discouragement and disappointment?
- What are some of the things in life that you have redefined as a result of disappointment? How have you redefined them, and what did you once believe them to be?

Root Problems

*See to it that no one
comes short of the grace of God;
that no root of bitterness springing up
causes trouble,
and by it many be defiled.*
Hebrews 12:15 (NASB)

God's grace or our bitterness, this is our decision.
God's grace for our bitterness, this is God's provision.

If you've ever had a lawn, you can relate to the problem of
dealing with weeds, especially dandelions. You know how tenacious
they are. If you let them go unattended, they quickly propagate
themselves causing even more trouble.

Years ago, in an attempt to get rid of some dandelions, I went
about plucking those suckers up wherever I found them in my lawn.
I called this the "pluck-'em-up" method. It was simple, quick and
easy. And sure enough, after a little plucking here and there, my
lawn looked great! But within a few days I noticed those dandelions
had sprouted right back up again. In some cases they came back
even bigger than before, and had multiplied! So, I went at it again,
this time with a little more gusto! I pulled those weeds with even
more determination. Yet, despite my added resolve, the "pluck-'em-
up" method provided no better solution the second time than the
first.

I soon realized that the "pluck-
'em-up" method had some major
shortcomings. For one, I found it
to be a lot of ongoing work and
maintenance. You see, I had
chosen this method in the first

*So the key is to get rid of
the roots.*

place because it worked with other weeds, like the ones you find in
your vegetable garden. But, for some reason, it didn't work with
dandelions. My question was, "why not?"

Well, as any lawn expert can tell you, it was because I wasn't dealing with the root of the problem, literally. You see, a dandelion puts down a deep taproot. If you just "pluck-'em-up" the upper part of the plant breaks-off while leaving the root system still in the ground. Though the leaves are gone and the lawn looks great, the roots are still very much alive. And it is from these roots that the plant sprouts again, and again, and again. So, the key is to get rid of the roots. If you don't, your only choices are to continue the "pluck-'em-up" method indefinitely, or just give up and let the dandelions do their thing.

As I began to think about this, I realized that dandelions are a lot like the problems we have in our lives. In our attempt to get rid of them, we often opt first for the "pluck-'em-up" method, which provides immediate results. However, we soon discover that

Roots are always at work, growing and sustaining the tree.

this fix is only temporary and those "dandelions" come right back. With this method we end up spending lots of time and energy trying to make things look good on the surface, while never really dealing with the roots. And in so doing, we always have to be on the alert for when the dandelions pop up again.

Often, we don't even realize that many of the hard issues we are dealing with come from a place of wounding hidden deep in our hearts. They spring from something buried below the surface, something we have forgotten, or something that we know about but don't want to look at. We doubt the good that can come from looking at the past. We question what we'd do with these old hurts even if we were to uncover them. Perhaps we have already tried to deal with "our stuff". Yet, we discovered that our attempts to do so, with the tools we had at the time, were ineffective. And really, who wants to go back and look at an issue only to feel the hurt all over again, especially when we fear there's no solution? It is at this point in most people's lives that denial looks really good.

However, drawing from my great wealth of experience with lawns, I believe I have found the keys to effectively dealing with the weeds—weeds in our lawns and weeds in our lives. It really all boils

A root of bitterness, it will do two things: cause trouble and defile many.

down to two things. First, we've got to eliminate the weeds--roots and all. Second, we've got to maintain a healthy, strong, weed-resistant lawn with good old-fashioned sun, water, and fertilizer.

Pray Through It

You see, a healthy lawn minimizes the growth of new weeds. It crowds them out—offers them no room. But perhaps more importantly, when we eliminate the weeds from the root level, the chances of old weeds returning is greatly reduced, if not nullified all together. Here lies the primary focus of this book, how to deal with the weeds in our lives-- roots and all.

Hebrews 12:15 speaks to this very issue. It basically says that if we allow in ourselves a root of bitterness, it will do two things-- cause trouble (like the recurring problems we struggle with), and defile many. No one likes to be around a bitter person, so it is easy to understand why bitterness would defile many. Bitter people tend to be irritating and negative. They easily get into arguments, and tend put others down. It takes a lot of effort to not let them affect you. It's hard not to react to a bitter person or, worse yet, become like them if you stay around them too long. And afterwards, it can take awhile to shake off their influence.

Roots

What I have noticed is that there are some key characteristics to roots. For one, obviously, they are buried beneath the surface, hidden from view. Because we don't see them, we don't think about them. We rarely consider the impact they are making. Because we tend to focus on what is visible, it is no wonder that roots are often overlooked. I don't know of anyone who says, "Hey, let's go to the forest to look at the roots!"

It takes work to remove roots.

A second characteristic about roots is that they are always at work, growing and sustaining the plant they belong to. Since they are covered up, you can't see all the directions they travel in. Nor can you see how large they are, or what they are doing. Yet, the evidence of their existence is seen above the surface—in the plant, itself, its leaves and its fruit. Without the roots, the plant would wither and die.

None of us would argue that because one can't see the roots of a tree they do not exist. Nor would anyone deny that the roots of a tree aren't doing anything just because you cannot see them. Yet, like Shawn, when it comes to our past, how often have we assumed that just because we are not aware of it, it isn't affecting us? Just because we aren't thinking about hurtful memories we assume they have no influence over us. Some of us even think that by keeping them buried we can somehow stop them from affecting us. But the truth is, though the roots are buried, they remain alive and active— an unseen force feeding the tree, or weeds, and causing it to grow.

A third characteristic about roots is that it takes work to remove them. You can't just ignore them and hope they'll go away. You have to dig if you want to find and get rid of them. You may even get a little dirty! Sometimes it will take a lot of work. And when you really get into it, you may need to put some other things on hold for awhile. But don't let that discourage you, because by not digging them up, you'd be doing more than just ignoring them—you'd actually be encouraging them to grow.

When you start digging around you may discover many things that have been hidden, forgotten and buried. Part of this work is being willing to deal with whatever you find along the way. And trust me, if you start digging, you *will* find things, good and bad. The good you want to keep. But the bad you will need to address if you want to experience lasting change. In the long run, it is well worth it.

Some assume that unless they *feel* something concerning their past, it has no relevancy or effect on the present. What they don't realize is that bitterness, resentment, hatred, and the like are not merely feelings but choices. So, even though a feeling may dissipate over time, when resentment is involved a choice has been made, and consequences are set in motion. These consequences are what the Bible refers to as "trouble" and "the defilement of others". It is misleading to assume that feelings are the only evidence as to whether or not a past hurt is relevant to what we are experiencing in our present.

We are neither to be ruled by nor are we to ignore our feelings.

I have been surprised to find out how many hurts in my past became rooted in resentment and bitterness without my conscious knowledge of it. Upon recalling some of those times, I did feel a measure of sadness and anger. Yet for others, I didn't actually *feel* anything. However, when I prayed through those memories (acknowledging that perhaps I had been bitter because the patterns in my life indicated it), I experienced a change. This verified that I actually *had* sown bitterness in my past, despite my inability to feel it.

Take for instance Shawn, in the beginning story. At first, he was unaware that he was bitter about some of the things in his past. He was very much in touch with his feelings of hurt towards his girlfriend, but those seemed to be the only "feelings" he was aware of. When he reflected on similar times in his past, he thought initially they were no big deal. He actually thought he had probably forgiven his offenders in those circumstances because he felt no ill

Pray Through It

will towards them. But upon praying through them, the results confirmed that he indeed had been harboring bitterness deep inside toward those people. And, in finally releasing them through prayer, he was able to embrace the healing and freedom he was seeking for his troubles in the present.

It is important that we listen to our feelings (Proverbs 4:23; Luke 6:45), though we are not to be ruled by them. Our feelings (or the lack of them) are merely indicators, like gauges in a car. They provide us feedback and information. They tell us something important is going on and give us warnings. We are

Once the lies get lodged in our heart, our heart will respond out of those beliefs.

neither to be ruled by them nor are we to ignore them. In actuality, our mind and our heart need to work together.

As with Shawn, there was a lie lodged in his heart that he was never good enough. All it took was for someone to imply that he was not good enough and he would be tempted to over-react. This over-reaction was an indicator that led us to consider there might be a deeper issue worth investigating.

Whenever we over-react, inevitably our feelings are involved. Such over-reactions are usually based upon lies—lies about what we believe concerning ourselves, our expectations, our needs, and who we are. Such beliefs as "nobody loves me" or, "I can't expect good things to happen to me," are examples of this.

These lies may also involve what we believe about others, such as "all men are jerks." Or they may involve our view about life, such as "life is unfair." It is in hurtful circumstances that we tend to give-in to such lies. What most of us don't realize, is that these lies take root because of our sinful responses to hurts from the past. Once the lies get lodged in our hearts, our hearts start interpreting our experiences through them. And out of these we respond.

Just because I am no longer in touch with the bitterness of yesterday doesn't mean it will not produce problems.

So, it would stand to reason that by changing our beliefs, our feelings should change as well. If this is true, then why does simply believing differently seem to work in some areas but not in others? Why does applying oneself through discipline and endurance bring about some measure of change, at some times, and yet at other times seem ineffective? One reason is because we need to *make choices* in keeping with these beliefs by taking action. Along with holding to a right belief system, we need to apply effort in breaking the bad habits while working to create good ones.

However, when it comes to *lies* lodged in the heart, often we need to go a step deeper. You see, when it's a lie we're dealing with we find our heart beliefs keep reverting back to the lie despite our self-discipline and better choices. In such instances, we need to take into account that this is possibly due to hidden bitterness which was our response to a time when we were hurt. It is the lack of healing and forgiveness in that area that keeps perpetuating the lie. The lie in turn continues to feed our hurt, not allowing a lasting change to come. No amount of head knowledge will change one's heart where bitterness holds it fast. Head knowledge is definitely useful for identifying the lies in our heart. And, it definitely helps us when wrestling against them. But, true change in the heart will only come by uncovering the root issues of bitterness and dealing with them.

I have heard it said, "Oh, what happened to me was so long ago," as if the further we distance ourselves from our past, the less it affects us. Yet, the past is just the past, whether it was twenty

*Time provides an opportunity
to deal with things.*

seconds or twenty years ago. The only difference is, a twenty-year-old root of bitterness has had more time to grow and produce troubles than a twenty-second-old one. Just because I am no longer in touch with the bitterness of yesterday, doesn't mean it will not produce troubles today, or in the near future for that matter.

I'm sure you've heard the old saying, "time heals all wounds". But, I have found this isn't exactly true. A wound *can* heal over time, if there is nothing to perpetuate its condition (like bitterness). In some cases, a wound can also get *worse* if it is not properly attended. Yet, with the proper care, under the right conditions, a wound is almost *guaranteed* to heal. Proper attention and care promotes the healing.

When it comes to denial, time only distances us from our past. Time may seem to have allowed us to outrun or stay ahead of our unhealed pain, but eventually it catches up to us.

What time can also do is to provide us an opportunity to deal with things. But it is up to us to do so. I would encourage you to take the time to consider the "weeds" in your life, and see if perhaps they might indeed be connected to a "root of bitterness."

Trouble

Pray Through It

Years ago, I used to help my father cut firewood. In his yard he had lots of different types of trees including several very large eucalyptus. These trees were fast-growing and did well in dry, hot climates. However, one of the problems or "troubles" with eucalyptus trees was that they would shed lots of bark and leaves, which would cover the ground. The result was that they made it very difficult for other plants to grow underneath them. It was not uncommon to see absolutely barren ground under these trees.

When converting a eucalyptus tree into firewood, we would cut down the entire tree, leaving only the base of the trunk. Now, you'd think after doing this the tree would just die. But these trees had a uncanny ability to sprout new branches from the stump which would eventually grow an entire new tree! And, if left alone, that new tree would grow even bigger than before! Why? Because the roots were not removed.

Now concerning firewood, this was great. We had a renewable source of fuel! But, if our goal was to get rid of the tree so we could plant other things in the surrounding soil, this method was sorely lacking.

This is not unlike the roots of bitterness that keep springing up in our lives, causing trouble. Like the discarded bark and leaves, do you find your own personal growth being hindered by the troubles in

"Troubles" can sometimes be the product of a root of bitterness-- the result of our sinful response to a hurtful situation.

your life? Do you find that you thought you had gotten rid of one issue only to see it sprout up again?

According to Strong's Dictionary the word "trouble" in Hebrews 12:15 means "to crowd in, annoy." I can sure relate to that definition. This is especially true when it comes to those recurring, negative circumstances that affect my finances, my work, and my relationships. And then there are those *people* in our lives. . .we all have them. . . people who cause trouble, who defile, who somehow seem to be able to bring out the worst in us--people who wear a dark cloud over their heads wherever they go.

These types of troubles crowd into our lives, consuming our time, energy and resources. They distract us from the things we really need and want to be attending to. And, they don't seem to go away despite our great efforts in dealing with them. Worse yet, we even come to anticipate and dread them because they're such a constant presence in our lives.

As Hebrews 12:15 points out, our "troubles" can often be the product of a root of bitterness-- the result of our sinful response to a hurtful situation. They are the result, or "fruit" which is produced.

When we think of the word "fruit", we usually think of things like apples and oranges. Yet the word "fruit" is not limited to this usage. In the broader sense, it refers to what is being produced or reproduced. It is the result of one's efforts and actions. It is the product produced from a particular source.

Good fruit comes from good roots, but bad fruit comes from bad roots.

The "troubles", mentioned in Hebrews 12:15, are what we would call "bad fruit". These are the things being produced in one's life that are related to a root of bitterness. Good fruit comes from good roots, but bad fruit comes from bad roots.

Is every trouble caused by a root of bitterness? The answer is a resounding "no". Troubles occur in our lives for a number of reasons. God may be allowing certain difficulties in order to build character, or challenge and develop us. Sometimes we are just in the right place at the wrong time or the wrong place at the right time. Sometimes we make poor choices. (For instance, if you don't spend money wisely, you won't be able to pay your bills.) We live in a fallen world and so we are likely to experience things that are in keeping with that.

Sometimes we create our own troubles and sometimes others create them for us. Regardless of the reason, God wants us to learn to respond to them rightly, trusting and seeking Him while growing in maturity.

The good news is, there are some key indicators which reveal whether the "trouble" in question stems from a root of bitterness or not. Once you know and understand these indicators you will find them tremendously helpful. We'll discuss them in detail later.

So what is bitterness, exactly? Bitterness is basically a form of unforgiveness. It is a choice--an unwillingness to forgive someone. When we choose to withhold forgiveness, we become bitter. We become unable to properly process and release our grief. In so doing, we become "stuck" in the hurt-- the pain remains in and with us. Despite our attempts to manage it, ignore it, deny it, medicate it, or let time heal it, it just doesn't go away. It becomes an annoyance, always there just under the surface. It becomes a sore spot, like a deep bruise on our arm. All it takes is for someone to bump us in the right spot, and we feel the pain. "Ouch!"—we react! They did not cause the bruise. It was already there. All they did was brush us the wrong way, but oh, how it hurt! It felt just like the original injury. Not quite as severe perhaps, but very reminiscent of our initial trauma!

Most of us are not even aware of the true origin of our pain, or the initial trauma. In fact, in most cases we are very much *unaware* that the pain we feel when someone brushes us the wrong way is in fact connected to our past. So, what our heart does is project what we are feeling onto what is tangible at the moment. Usually, this is the present offender, such as our boss, our spouse, the kids, the dog, etc.

When we are triggered in this manner, we often respond without thinking, we over-react. We may become defensive, or withdraw. We may flee. We may even turn to addiction in an attempt to find temporary relief. In all these things our unresolved past now becomes a poison affecting not only us but also everyone around us. All it takes is for something to tap into our pain, something to hook us, and often without knowing it, the evidence of the bitter root's existence manifests through our reaction.

Here's something to consider when you see an over-reaction in yourself. Ask yourself, "Could it be that the trouble, the bad fruit, I am experiencing in my life is related to a root of bitterness?

Defilement

Now there is another thing that occurs whenever there is a root of bitterness. Hebrews 12:15 says that it has the capacity to "defile many". The word "defile" means "to sully or taint; to contaminate" (Strong's Dictionary, 1890). Often, when we think of "defilement", we think of its most common usage-- people's behavior or words affecting us by tainting or contaminating our thoughts. We feel polluted by what someone else says or does—hearing off-color jokes or conversation, listening to gossip, watching a vulgar or lustful movie, even listening to certain music. It's like someone putting a big, filthy blanket on us. I call it "getting spiritually dirty".

An analogy for "defiling many" would be like my being covered with grease and then giving someone a hug or a handshake. Some people would be immediately repulsed and step back, not even letting me give them a hug or shake their hand. As a result I might feel rejected. For others, they might actually let me hug them but then they are left to figure out how to get the grease off. They might later react by getting mad at me. They might even be gruff or speak meanly of me behind my back. But, then there are others still, who are covered with grease themselves. They don't mind hanging with me because, after all, "misery loves company"—and we have our defilement in common.

Sometimes defilement is not a tangible thing. That is, it's not necessarily associated with someone's direct actions or words.

Sometimes it's simply a sense of being dirtied by someone's presence and attitude. We find ourselves feeling like there is just something about them that affects us in a negative way. This "something about them" is what tempts us to react inappropriately toward them. Perhaps we are tempted to reject them or treat them in some negative way. It is as if the worst is being drawn out of us. What defilement does is tempt us to treat the person with it in a manner that is in keeping with their root of bitterness. This works both ways, for my defilement tempts others to react to me in a way that is in keeping with my roots.

You may know someone that seems to invite rejection wherever they go. Or, maybe you know someone who somehow always draws

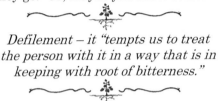

Defilement – it "tempts us to treat the person with it in a way that is in keeping with root of bitterness."

the wrong kind of attention, whether they are looking for it or not. You may remember feeling tempted to respond in kind though it wouldn't be your intention to do so.

I remember a woman who was seeking help and prayer for some bad fruit in her life. At one point in our initial time together, I found myself wanting to be sarcastic with her, which was certainly not the appropriate thing to be doing. I had to repeatedly make a choice to ignore this impulse. As it turned out, I soon discovered she had been wounded by sarcasm growing up. Once I realized this, it made sense. I was being tempted by the defilement of her bitterness towards those who had hurt her in this way before. This also let me know what types of issues she needed to pray through.

Another time, I remember getting into an argument with a man during our ministry time together. He got very heated up trying to defend something that wasn't true. Yet, the more I tried to show him his error, the more heated the argument became. Despite providing solid evidence, he just got madder and more insistent. It was at this point that I realized that I had been yielding to his defilement. So I said, "You know what? *You* are much more important than winning an argument." The next thing that happened was that he started sharing how his father would never let him win an argument. Just like that, we found the root cause of his defilement. And yes, we prayed through it. . .

While ministering to a certain woman years ago, I found myself talking on and on while she listened attentively. I found it very appealing to do this. She was a great listener! Yet, I sensed that something was not quite right. *She* needed to be listened to. *She* was the one who had come for ministry, not me. So, I stopped and asked her if she typically found herself doing all the listening. She

Pray Through It

said, "Yes, but I don't mind." Here she had become so accustomed to others doing all the talking and she do the listening, that it had become normal for her. Out of her past hurt, she had taken on the role of being the listener. And I, too, had fallen into the expectations of her defilement.

Defilement of this sort is not intentional. The person is not trying to tempt others to respond in a manner in keeping with their roots. Rather, defilement is a product of having a root of bitterness; it occurs naturally.

What is important to keep in mind is that it is not right for us to blame others for our wrong behavior when we feel defiled by them. Instead, we need to consider what it is in us which allows their defilement to tempt us to react as such.

Often, the harder we find it is to resist one's defilement, the bigger the issue is in us that needs to be addressed. Recognizing this allows us to see these times as an opportunity to deal with our own issues. By recognizing our reaction for what it is, and then identifying its root source, we can then pray through it. In so doing, we can then work towards minimizing our vulnerability to another's defilement.

I want to emphasize that defilement from others doesn't *make* us respond in a certain way. It merely *tempts* us to do so. The same is true for us-- we do not *make* others treat us in a certain way. Our defilement only *tempts* them to respond as they do. You and I are responsible for our own actions and reactions, despite anyone's defilement.

I sometimes think of defilement as being like "push buttons" that we wear. Each button has a different label. One may say, "I don't need anybody", another says, "Nobody loves me" and so on. Each label refers to a specific defilement. The labels are the lies that we have come to believe about ourselves, about others, and about life. When someone

You and I are responsible for our own actions and reactions, despite anyone's defilement.

does something that is in keeping with one of those labels, it's just like they push one of our buttons. This then brings up the pain associated with that button, which tempts us to react in some sort of inappropriate way.

Imagine two people standing in front of each other with buttons all over them. At some point, for whatever reason, one pushes the other's button. The other feels hurt and then reacts by pushing one of the buttons on the first person. The next thing we have is a "button-pushing battle". Sound familiar? Feel familiar?

In the heat of battle, it seems our only options are to keep pushing the other person's buttons or retreat. This is why we may find ourselves wanting to avoid certain people—to keep from getting in a "button-pushing battle" with them. But really the problem is not so much with the other person, as irritating as they might be. And the problem is not so much with us, it's *within* us. If only we could disconnect our buttons we would be less likely to react the way we do. You see, we can't always change our circumstances, but we can change ourselves.

Just as it takes two people to dance, it takes only one person to stop the dancing. This is accomplished both in "button-pushing

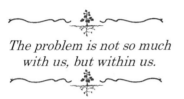

The problem is not so much with us, but within us.

battles" and dancing by dealing with ourselves and own root issues first, instead of attacking the other person and insisting that they be the ones to change.

By getting rid of the defilement in our hearts, we can effect real change in our relationships. And even if the people around us never change, we can at least find ourselves responding differently to them. Through prayer and forgiveness we can find the freedom to speak up or leave, without feeling like we used to. We have freedom to take the time to actually think before responding inappropriately. We can feel less vulnerable and more secure, less controlled and more confident. Though we may still be tempted from time to time to react in old ways, dealing with temptation won't be as difficult as it once was. And, we can begin to see our lives through a new set of glasses—ones that aren't tainted by our negative expectations. Through new eyes we'll be able to see those who once opposed us more as God sees them.

God's Grace

In Hebrews 12:15, we are encouraged not to miss out on God's grace. What is important to recognize is that the missing out on, and the receiving of, God's grace is up to us—not God. He's made His grace available. It's up to us to receive it. So how is it we miss out? Well, before answering that, we need to know the purpose of God's grace.

God's grace has many purposes and many applications. Concerning the focus of this book, we will look specifically at two of those purposes. The first is that God poured out His grace to restore our relationship with Him. This was done through overcoming the sin that separated us from Him. Bottom line, He wants an intimate relationship with us.

Another purpose for God's grace is to stop the on-going production of bad fruit in our lives. Through the cross, He put to death the reaping of death as the penalty for our sins.

Through counseling and introspection we might be able to figure out some of the original life-situations which tempted us to believe lies about ourselves, others and life itself. Yet what good is that if we are not able to undo the bad cycles they have set in motion? Understanding alone does not heal the past-- neither can it remove its defiling influence. Simply trying harder, being more disciplined and making positive affirmations won't heal the past either. These tools are useful for shaping change, but they cannot remove the poisoning effects the past has on the present. Even resorting to denial or renunciation of the past won't help.

God's grace is able to stop the production of bad fruit in our lives.

It is only by God's grace, and applying the very real work of the cross, that we are able to stop the production of bad fruit in our lives. And how do we actually do that? How do we receive that grace and apply it towards the healing of our root issues?

Since it was our sinful responses that started the bearing of bad fruit in the first place, it is our sinful responses that need to be rooted out. This is done by receiving the grace made available to us, by confessing our specific sinful responses to what happened to us, forgiving those who hurt us, and then renouncing the lies and vows we came to own in response to that hurt. It is when we *don't* do this that we end up "missing out".

Things to Cultivate

- In what areas have you been finding yourself doing a lot of ongoing maintenance just to keep your attitudes and behavior in check?
- Are there some areas that you have decided to just "let time heal"? If so, what are they? Has time really healed them?
- In what areas do you find yourself over-reacting or under-reacting (withdrawing, being passive)? Give an example of when this happened.
- What are some examples of when you have experienced defilement or felt tempted to react to someone in a manner inconsistent with your usual behavior?

Sowing and Reaping

Do not be deceived: God cannot be mocked.
A man reaps what he sows.
The one who sows to please his sinful nature, from that nature will
reap destruction; the one who sows to please the Spirit, from the
Spirit will reap eternal life.
Let us not become weary in doing good, for at the proper time we
will reap a harvest if we do not give up.
Galatians 6:7-9

Sowing and reaping was God's idea.

Obviously, God had a wonderful purpose for sowing and reaping, for God is good. He reveals a part of who He is through what He does and creates. Sowing and reaping reveal God's generosity and goodness, His desire to reward us. It's God's nature to bless, and He wants to bless us. It is His desire that we bear good fruit resulting from our choices, actions, words and thoughts. During creation He gave the command and blessing to, "Be fruitful and multiply" (Genesis 1:22, 28; 9:7). This has been His desire and purpose from the very beginning.

From the beginning, the world was a place where, no matter what a person did, they would reap in return. This was God's incentive program--rewarding us for our efforts, encouraging us to create and explore.

But when Adam and Eve disobeyed God, sin entered on to the scene. The principle of sowing and reaping was still in effect, but now the reaping could come from good or from evil. A sin nature (Romans 7:5ff) was added in to the equation, and ever since that time humans have been struggling with that tendency, that temptation, to sin. Every time we make choices from our sin nature, we reap bad fruit. When we make choices in keeping with what it right and good, we reap good fruit. If you are like me, I don't mind reaping good fruit. It's the reaping of bad fruit that concerns me. Thankfully, God has provided the perfect means by which we can put an end to the bad while still reaping the good.

Pray Through It

By the way, to not reap is not an option. Even if we sow nothing, we reap nothing. So the question is: what will we sow – good or bad?

Since sowing and reaping is so important we need to know what it means. We each "sow" in whatever we do, such as in our actions, words or thoughts. We "reap" when the product of what we have sown returns to us. The reaping may not be immediate, but it is guaranteed. This is why we are encouraged not to "...become weary

So the question is: what will we sow – good or bad?

in doing good, for at the proper time we will reap a harvest if we do not give up" (Galatians 6:9).

Sir Isaac Newton's "Third Law of Motion" is an example of the principle of sowing and reaping. It states as that "for every action, there is an equal and opposite reaction." As a result of this law, scientists can often predict results from a given set of conditions. In addition, they can use this principle in the reverse. They can often deduce the prior conditions based upon the resultant reactions. In this way, they can "work" the equation in both directions. This allows for a certain amount of predictability, allowing one to determine the cause that resulted from the effect. And so it is with the principle of sowing and reaping.

The principle of sowing and reaping is found throughout Scripture as well. The following are just a few examples:

Judging

Judge not lest you be judged.
Matthew 7:1 (NASB)

Don't pick on people, jump on their failures, criticize their faults--unless, of course, you want the same treatment.
Matt. 7:1 (MSG)

For in the way you judge, you will be judged; and by your standard of measure, it will be measured to you. And why do you look at the speck that is in your brother's eye, but do not notice the log that is in your own eye? Or how can you say to your brother, "Let me take the speck out of your eye," and behold, the log is in your own eye? You hypocrite, first take the log out of your own eye, and then you will see clearly to take the speck out of your brother's eye.
Matthew 7:2-5 (NASB)

This portion of Scripture makes it clear that it can be okay to judge, but *only under certain circumstances.* For judgment to be pure and undefiled, it is to come from a place of compassion and concern coupled with personal purity and humility, rather than from a place of condemnation. This is important, since there are specific consequences that will occur if these conditions are not first met.

When we judge, we do so based upon our understanding of right and wrong. But God tells us that our judgment *will be* impaired if we are in denial about something or have not dealt with sin in our own lives first. This is what the scriptures call "the log" in our own eyes. Often, this is the very thing that tempts us to condemn others in a certain area. Sometimes "the log" in our own eye is a previous judgment against someone that had hurt us. So now when we feel treated in a similar way by another person, we are unable to see the situation clearly since our previous issue is being stirred up.

Our condemnation of others ends up coming back on us.

Consider this point too, why would someone even allow us to point out something in their life, if we are in denial about the same issue in our own? What credibility would we have? Therefore, when we judge another before we have examined ourselves first, what we reap is our own judgment upon ourselves. In essence, our condemnation of others ends up coming back on us.

A very common scenario I have seen is when, as a child, someone makes a vow out of unforgiveness and hurt such as, "I'm *never* going to be like my father (or mother) when I grow up!" Now, there may have been some wisdom in that decision, because their parent may have been cruel and abusive. But, because this decision was made from a place of unforgiveness, it backfires. The bad fruit shows up when that person is in a situation or role similar to the conditions of that early decision. Ironically, they end up either acting just like or just the polar opposite of that person. They fly to the extreme, one way or the other. Condemnation comes over them whenever they do something that is just like their father (or mother). If they resist the urge to be abusive, they often become passive. And neither extreme bears good fruit. These are the people who live in a place of dismay wondering how it is they could've failed when they vowed so hard not to.

In my case, because I had judged my father's wrongful use of authority and made the vow to never become like him, I reaped passivity. It was as if my heart was holding me back for fear that I might be condemned for doing anything that even looked like him. I was afraid to use my authority at all, even in the right ways. I became apologetic in my directives toward others. There was a lack of strength in my decision making, causing them to feel insecure with my leadership. I also came across unsure of myself and hesitant, too afraid of offending anyone.

The good part is, once one prays through such past vows and decisions, they are free to keep the wisdom of those early decisions while not being bound to the condemnation of them. They can forgive the offender and move on to walk in the fullness of life as it is intended to be. Since doing this myself, I have found that I am able to walk in my authority as a man in a healthy way, without fear and without condemnation.

<u>Honoring Parents</u>

"Honor your father and mother"
— which is the first commandment with a promise—'that it may go
well with you and that you may enjoy long life on the earth.
Ephesians 6:2-3

Notice that honoring one's parents contains a promise. If honor is given (that's the sowing), life will go well (the reaping). Yet the opposite is also true. Where we did *not* honor our parents, life will *not* go well for us. So let's consider those areas where life might not be going well with us. Did we perhaps dishonor our parents in those areas? And if so, how?

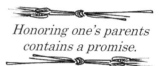

Honoring one's parents contains a promise.

One way we dishonor our parents is through our attitudes, such as hatred, bitterness, cursing, etc. Essentially, this is done through holding unforgiveness towards them. Now that we are older we may not even realize or remember holding such attitudes against them in the past. Or, we may think that though we did at one time, it's really not an issue anymore. Yet, the fruit in our lives may be a strong indicator that we do, in fact, have unforgiveness about something.

I have met people who struggle in their finances-- there never seems to be enough money. Despite their efforts to work hard, apply good financial advice, and not be like their family of origin, nothing seems to make a difference. Even when they finally succeed in earning a little extra money, it's not enough. Though there may be other reasons, in some instances we discovered that what was happening was rooted in resentment towards their parents for "never having enough". For example, as a child they saw money being wasted on alcohol or mismanagement. This was money that could have been used to buy decent clothes or do nice things on the holidays, or even buy food. Yet, it was diverted to other things and therefore they never felt like they had enough as a child.

Finances are just one area where life might not go well. There are a host of others like relationships, marriage, work, personal recognition, etc. Unforgiveness, and hence dishonor, toward one's parents can affect all these things. But we can reverse the bad fruit of dishonor by choosing to forgive. Forgiveness changes our history of dishonoring into a new attitude of honoring, thus allowing life from that point forward to go well, at least in those specific areas.

Giving

Give, and it will be given to you.
A good measure, pressed down, shaken together and running over,
will be poured into your lap. For with the measure you use, it will be
measured to you.
Luke 6:38

When we think of giving, we often think of things we can do, such the giving of our time, energy, resources and encouragement. We also give when we love someone, listen to them or defend them. Luke 6:38 promises that giving (sowing) assures an eventual return (reaping), and that with an increase.

But the act of giving is not limited to good things only. What if we give things like broken promises, a merciless attitude, cheap presents, leftover time, lies, betrayal, or flattery? What can we expect in return? Again, the manner in which you sow, will be the manner in which you reap.

The Spirit vs. The Flesh

The one who sows to please his sinful nature,
from that nature will reap destruction;
the one who sows to please the Spirit,
from the Spirit will reap eternal life.
Galatians 6:8

This verse is very straightforward--we sow either to our sin nature or to the Spirit, and we reap in kind. I am so glad that God made a provision to deal with what we have sown to our sin nature!

The previous examples are but a few of the places in Scripture that illustrate the principle of sowing and reaping. The following are some others you can look up for yourself: Deuteronomy 28; Psalms 126:5-6; Proverbs 22:8; Jeremiah 4:3; Hosea 8:7; Matthew 25:14-30; I Corinthians 9:11 & 15:42-44; and James 3:18. You may also want to take a closer look at the entire book of Proverbs. In many places, though the words "sowing" and "reaping" are not specifically used, the principle is definitely there.

Pray Through It

Seed Sowing

Now, try and imagine all the things you have done and are going to do (whether they be actions, words or thoughts) as seeds. Every time you do something, it's like planting one of those seeds. And every time you plant one of those seeds, it then germinates and eventually sprouts. And when it does, it does so after its *own kind*, depending upon the type of seed that was planted. As time goes on, the plant will grow and produce fruit. Some plants mature early, others take longer--but inevitably you reap something. And this "something" is in keeping with the type of seed that was planted. Or in this case, the type of thing you did.

One result of the plant produced is, of course, more seeds—*lots* more seeds, which produce future plants, promising an increase. This is the cycle of sowing and reaping. And all of this results from the planting of just a few little seeds. So it is with our actions, words and thoughts.

For instance, someone may reject us in some certain way which, of course, hurts. Now, if we have a pre-existing root issue around rejection, then it

...our sin nature actually feeds upon hidden resentments and roots of bitterness.

will hurt even more. If rejection continues to come our way, the lies in our heart around that issue increase as we continue to respond negatively. Soon, we start taking on other lies. It may start simply with the belief that "no one likes me", but then we add to it the lie that "something is wrong with me." To this, we later add "I'm bad" and then "I don't need anybody." This is where the increase happens—where "insult is added to injury"—and all of this originating from a tiny little root of bitterness around rejection. Soon the list of those who we feel have rejected us has increased as well. Maybe we even come to believe that God has rejected us, too.

Such things as bitterness, dishonor, resentment and condemnation are the kind of bad seeds we are easily tempted to sow. We can also add to this list hatred, despising, vengeance, and cursing. These are some of the possible responses we may have had to hurtful situations often involving another individual and their impact on our real, felt, and perceived needs. These are sinful choices often backed by very strong feelings. When we don't deal with them, we are choosing to hold unforgiveness towards those involved.

What we may not realize is that often our sin nature actually feeds upon hidden resentments and roots of bitterness. As roots bring nourishment to a tree, so our roots of bitterness "nourish" our sin nature. As we rid our hearts of these things, our sin nature has less to draw upon. While we are in these bodies we will always have to battle our sin nature. But, the battle can be made less fierce if we deprive our sin nature of the food it loves—unconfessed sin, lies, and bitterness. On the one hand, this may explain some of the difficulties we may be having, yet on the other, we cannot let this become an excuse to continue in our sin.

Further, it is good to keep in mind that not everything that happens to us is a result of sowing and reaping. Sometimes, the Lord allows things in our lives in order to build

Not everything that happens to us is a result of our sowing and reaping.

character, to teach us, to let us see our potential, to bring out the best in us, and to encourage us to seek Him and go deeper in our relationship with Him. Some things are just natural events beyond our control. Some are the consequences of the choices others have made. Again, we need to keep in mind that we have a sin nature which we alone are responsible to contend with. We also have an enemy who, from time to time, we have to resist in battle. No matter what the cause of our present struggles, God wants us to look to Him and to learn whatever it is He is trying to teach us. I am very thankful that His grace keeps us from reaping more than we already have (or perhaps should) and that it is sufficient for us, no matter what the circumstance.[1]

In some cases, we may have been truly victimized at some point, but we do not have to remain victims. Some of us may want to blame our past (or people in our past) for our present problems. And, yes, often those experiences were very difficult and hurtful. Our needs may not have been honored or met. We may have

What happened in our past is not so much the problem as what our response to it was.

been violated, harmed or neglected, and it may have affected us very deeply.

Yet, what actually happened to us is not so much the problem as what our response was to it. The problem is not so much our past but that we blamed our past, or rather those in it. If we have blamed others and held them in unforgiveness, we remain vulnerable to them and people like them, as well as experiences that make us feel that same way again. If it was rejection, then rejection

---

[1] 2 Corinthians 12:9 says: "But he said to me, 'My grace is sufficient for you, for my power is made perfect in weakness.' Therefore I will boast all the more gladly about my weaknesses, so that Christ's powers may rest on me." The word "weakness" in Greek refers not to Paul's "sinful infirmities (those he had reason to be ashamed of…) but to his afflictions, necessities, persecutions and distresses for the sake of Christ." (Matthew Henry's Commentary)

becomes a target within us—not because we were rejected, but *because of our sinful response* to those who rejected us. Any new rejection we experience will seem to have excellent aim in striking that target and bringing up that initial pain all over again.

Bad experiences in our past don't always result in bad fruit.

Having said this, I also need to emphasize that not all bad experiences result in bad fruit. If we, by God's grace, didn't make any sinful responses during a negative or hurtful time, then there won't be any bad fruit later on. And, even if we did have an initial sinful response to what happened, as long as we dealt with it right away, then it won't bear bad fruit either. If this were not so, we would all be trapped as victims of the past. We would be stuck, believing there was nothing we could do about it. This type of thinking would lead us to feel like hostages of the past, prisoners of those who hurt us. And, that somehow unless they were to release us, repent, ask us for forgiveness, give us what we need or receive the punishment we feel is due, we could not break free.

Thankfully, I am so glad that it's not this way. By choosing to forgive our offenders, at *any* point in our lives, and by receiving forgiveness for our response to the initial hurt, we invite and allow God to come in and redeem the past. This is where He loves to turn ashes into beauty—to make a testament to His glory and power. And, this is where His glory is made manifest in us through the mercy and grace expressed by His shed blood.

Things to Cultivate

- In the world around you, in what ways have you observed the principle of sowing and reaping?
- In what ways have you seen the judging of another come back on someone?
- What are some areas in your life that are not going well? Could these possibly be related to dishonoring your father and mother in some way?
- What are some of the areas where you experience the most difficulty in wrestling with your sin nature? Could this be related to a root case? If so, what do you think it might be?
- What are some things you have blamed others for?
- Describe some times when you experienced God's grace as being sufficient in your weakness?

Characteristics of Reaping

For nothing is hidden that shall not become evident, nor anything secret that shall not be known and come to light.
Luke 8:17 (NASB)

The sins of some men are quite evident, going before them to judgment; for others, their sins follow after.
Likewise also, deeds that are good are quite evident, and those which are otherwise cannot be concealed.
1 Tim 5:24-25 (NASB)

God's plan is for all things to become evident.

So, what evidence can help us distinguish troubles that are the result of "sowing and reaping" versus those that are not? What should we be looking for in order to help us tell the difference?

The thing about seeds is that once planted, though initially hidden, they will in time give evidence to their existence when they sprout. They cannot remain hidden forever. When they do sprout, they, themselves, eventually show us what type of seed was originally planted. And, if there is any question as to what species it is when the plant is immature, the resulting flower or fruit will provide the clinching testimony.

Likewise, knowing and understanding some key characteristics about sowing and reaping can be very helpful when sorting out troubles. This information will help us recognize the difference between which troubles in our lives are the result of "sowing and reaping" and which ones are not. Once we know what type of trouble we are dealing with, we will know what type of solution to apply.

From the scriptures, we are told of some key characteristics to look for concerning the "bearing of fruit". Let's take a look at these:

Fruitful – What type of fruit is being produced in my life?

Seasonal – What are the particular times and conditions under which the fruit is produced?
Persistent – What seems to persist in my life no matter what I do or don't do?
Increasing -- Is there an increase of this reaping in my life?

These characteristics are typical for most any fruit-bearing plant. Since we want to keep the good fruit and get rid of the bad, let's focus here on those things characteristic of the bearing of bad fruit.

Keep in mind that not all these traits need to be evident in order to label something as "bad fruit". Just as not all trees are at the same stage of development, so it is with the reaping in our lives. Some seeds may still be lying dormant, waiting for the right season (circumstances) before sprouting. Others have sprouted, but the type of fruit they will bear is not yet clear. Some have not or may

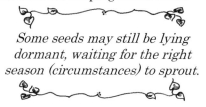

Some seeds may still be lying dormant, waiting for the right season (circumstances) to sprout.

not even make it to the stage of increase. But when the fruit is ripe, you'll know it. The important thing is recognizing something as bad fruit not matter what stage of development it is in so that we can begin to do something about it. Hence, we'll examine these characteristics a little more closely.

Fruitful

You will know them by their fruits. Grapes are not gathered from thorn bushes nor figs from thistles, are they?
Matt. 7:16 (NASB)

As in farming, if you sow kernels of corn, you get corn stalks. If you plant apple seeds, you get apple trees. The seeds you plant determine the type of fruit you will eventually reap. Therefore, if I

The fruit in our lives gives evidence to what type of seeds have been sown.

have weeds in my garden, I know what type of seeds they came from!

So it is with our lives. The fruit in our lives gives evidence to the type of seeds that have been sown. At some point, the fruit becomes ripe, or evident. When it's bad fruit, it is God's way of letting us know there are past unhealed issues which need to be addressed. This is

God's invitation and our opportunity to allow His grace to put an end to it.

When you get down to it, it's really is quite simple. If you have the fruit, then you have a root. And the root will look like the fruit. Thus, there is a certain amount of predictability when it comes to identifying the source of bad fruit in our lives. The root issues that brought about the bad fruit will be similar in appearance.

If you have bad fruit that manifests when you're around authority figures, then you will want to consider there are root issues behind it. It's possible that you may have made some judgments against authority figures in the past. Perhaps you have mistrust issues with the police, your boss, or your teachers. If so, it is likely you judged an earlier authority figure, such as one of your parents, as being harsh or untrustworthy. Since God is an authority figure you might even have difficulty trusting the Lord or hearing His voice concerning personal issues in your life.

One day I went out to the waiting room to greet a woman who had come seeking help with some issues. As I walked up to her, I sensed she held a strong belief that all men are jerks. Yet, she was very pleasant and never mentioned anything about that as being one of her presenting concerns. After about a half hour or so I took a chance and asked her if she felt that way—that all men are jerks. And, without hesitation she blurted out, "Why they all are, aren't they?!" I assured her that there were indeed some "non-jerks" in this world. And she responded, "Then where are they?"

I soon learned that wherever she went she experienced men who were disrespectful, uncaring and selfish. Whether she expected this, or looked for behavior that *appeared* as "jerkiness" and seized upon it, or somehow brought this out in men, her experiences were very much a part of her reality. As a result, it was difficult for her heart to believe that men could be anything but jerks. Because of her judgments, she regularly experienced the bad fruit of this in her life. And sure enough, this pointed to root issues around men in her past who had acted like jerks that she had in turn judged.

I also remember there being a time when I was uncomfortable with hugs and affection. Growing up, I just thought there were "huggy" families and "non-huggy" families, and ours was a "non-huggy" family. I don't remember ever resenting not getting hugs, so it was no big deal—or so I thought.

But one day, I began to recognize the importance of hugs. I came to see how hugs promote confidence and give reassurance; how they remove shame and make us feel accepted; how they help a person feel loved. So, I made a decision to attempt to give and receive hugs on a more regular basis. Yet, when I attempted to give or receive a hug, it was still very awkward and uncomfortable for me. I found myself wanting to give sideways hugs rather than a regular hug. Some friends even told me they could tell I was still resisting their hugs. Over time, I did get a bit more comfortable with the whole "hug thing". Yet, I just couldn't shake feeling of being mechanical. I finally came to the place of thinking that this might be bad fruit in my life, and that I should look deeper to see where it was rooted.

Seasonal

...for in due season we shall reap...
Galatians 6:9 (KJV)

Another characteristic to look at is the seasonality with which certain fruit is born. That is, if we study the bad fruit in our lives we will notice that it comes forth only in certain situations and only at certain times. And that those times have a habit of coming seasonally.

Where I live, there are farms we call "You-pick" farms. This is where the owners let customers come and pick their own fresh produce for a reduced price. One of the places we go provides a produce chart, which shows the anticipated dates when certain types of fruit and vegetables will be ripe for picking. For example, it shows that mid to late June is best for strawberries and mid July is best for cherries. Each fruit has its own season, and there's no messing with or changing the order in which those seasons come about. Some seasons are shorter than others. For instance, you have only a two-week window to pick cherries. Some seasons are year-round, like for the orange trees near my boyhood home in California.

The bearing of fruit in our lives has seasons as well.

Some fruit bearing seasons overlap one another, while others can actually shift depending upon the weather patterns for a given year. For instance, some fruits will only come if a growing season is long and hot, while others need to be preceded by a very cold winter. Did you know that there are certain pine trees whose seeds will not sprout unless there has been a fire?

Another thing is that some fruit trees take several years before they show any sign of bearing fruit. Meanwhile, they are growing and developing. So, it may take quite a few seasons before we see any fruit from them.

A characteristic about seasons is that they are cyclic. Every year, generally around the same time, each distinctive fruit- bearing plant or tree bears its fruit.

Have you ever found yourself saying, "Why does this always happen to me (whenever I start a new job, or get into a new relationship)?" or "Why do I keep doing that?" It's like you're caught in a cycle. And, if you notice, it seems to happen around the same set of circumstances. As a result, you may have begun to develop a cyclical expectation that something negative will happen, even before it does. This is a clue that root issues may be involved.

In some cases, seasons of bad fruit could come with a specific date on the calendar or a certain time of year, such as a birthday or anniversary. Perhaps every year your birthday keeps getting forgotten. Or, maybe your birthday isn't necessarily forgotten but always ends up being a disappointment. For some people, it might be a particular month or day when something terrible happened like a death or divorce. A common "bad-fruit-bearing-season" which I'm sure you've heard of is Christmas. What's important to investigate is what could have possibly happened on these dates in years past that caused so much hurt in the first place.

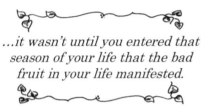

...it wasn't until you entered that season of your life that the bad fruit in your life manifested.

Of course, not all our seasons have to do with actual dates and times. Sometimes they involve the start of certain types of relationships, work circumstances or life transitions. For instance, these might be such things as getting married, having children, buying a home, starting a new job, and going to a new school, etc. How many times have we heard, "Everything seemed to change once we got married"? What happened was that it took entering the season of marriage (not "dating", not "living together") to bring forth issues which would not have manifested otherwise. The same is true with having children. Certain traits in you and certain issues from your past may not have surfaced until your first child was born. Sometimes it takes having a particular gender of child (i.e., a son versus a daughter, or visa versa) to bring out the bad fruit. In any case, it's not until you enter a very specific season that the bad fruit comes to the surface.

The season may also involve relationships with only certain types of people. For instance, the bad fruit may occur only when we are around women (or men). It may only happen when we are around passive personalities or in the presence of "control-freaks".

The season might be a particular circumstance--like being in front of a group, working on finances, or arguing. It may be in certain situations that require a response, like having to express feelings or make a decision. It might be at work versus at home, on vacation versus at the office.

Once identified, these seasons are a clue that can help us find the bitter root that needs healing in our past. The season that brought forth the present bad fruit is frequently similar to the season in the past where the original seed was sown.

As for me, being uncomfortable with giving hugs and receiving affection, the seasons were Sunday mornings at church and Bible study nights (when everyone is visiting and hugging and shaking hands). Whatever the specifics are for you, be it a certain date, situation, or type of person you meet up with, seasons can be a key indicator as to the bitter roots you might be looking for.

Persistent

They will plant wheat and reap weeds.
Nothing they do will work out.
They will look at their meager crops and wring their hands.
Jeremiah 12:13 (MSG)

As mentioned in a previous chapter, as long as I put off dealing with the roots, the dandelions in my lawn prevailed. All my previous efforts had been focused on dealing with what was being produced, what was evident or above the ground. Sure, by removing what was seen things looked great, but only for a little while. The dandelions persisted because my practical attempts did not get rid of the roots.

Perhaps you can relate to this in your own life. You have tried all sorts of methods to fix or get rid of the problems. And why not try them? These methods have been proven to work for other applications. Yet, no matter what you do it doesn't seem to be working in a lasting way. In cases such as these, it's time to consider that root issues may be the culprit.

You see, although there are some people who are adept at "managing" their bad fruit, they do so at the price of a tremendous output of energy and self-control—all of which is extremely wearying. They find themselves adjusting their lives and relationships in order to minimize the possibility of the bad fruit manifesting. And, in so doing, sacrifice the "abundant life" Jesus means for each of us to have.

I once met a businessman who had to put out five times the effort for three times the gain. A lot of his energy and effort went toward compensating and dealing with the distractions and set backs that kept coming his way. This may seem like a lot of work and frustration to you and me, yet for him, it was the only way he knew of to get ahead. And, it was better than doing nothing! Fortunately, he had a great deal of drive and determination. Not so for most of us

Some people may resort to spiritualizing their experience, calling it "spiritual warfare," "trials" or "bearing one's cross" when perhaps its not. Though at times one of these might indeed be involved or be the real issue, a root cause might be involved as well.

As for my issue with hugging, when I purposed put out effort to hug others, it did seem to help. Yet, despite my efforts it didn't change how I felt deep down inside. The awkward and mechanical feel about hugging persisted. The best I could do was to continue giving and receiving hugs, even though it didn't come naturally. On the surface it looked like things had changed, but underneath I knew I was still struggling.

Increasing

He produces a crop, yielding a hundred,
sixty or thirty times what was sown.
Matthew 13:23b

... but if it is buried, it sprouts
and reproduces itself many times over.
John 12:24b (MSG)

Whether it is corn or weeds, the goal of the seed is to "increase"-- to grow, to bear fruit and to reproduce itself. All it takes is time and the right conditions, and an increase will eventually result.

Take the woman who viewed all men as jerks. Early on in her life she had judged the first man she knew as a jerk. This was her father. For a while, he seemed to be the only jerk. But, then she met other men whose similar behavior reinforced

The goal of the seed is "increase"-- to grow,
to bear fruit and to reproduce itself.

what had been sown in her heart. And out of that place of pain, she was tempted to become more bitter towards men. She soon came to *expect* all men to act like jerks. As she continued on through life, things seemed to get worse and worse concerning the men she encountered. What started as a judgment against one man grew to be an attitude toward several men and then increased to become an expectation about all men. The seed brought about an increase.

It is not uncommon to see this go to the next level. When we enter into marriage we bring with us a lot of baggage-- good stuff worth keeping as well as a lot of rotten stuff which really needs to be thrown out. If a woman marries with a hidden root of bitterness that says "all men are jerks," it's likely she will marry a man who at times acts like a jerk. And if he doesn't, she will draw out or look for any "jerkiness" that happens to be in him. All of this comes from the lies lodged in her heart through past hurts that she begins acting upon. If they have children, it is likely the children will be tempted to judge their parents' behavior towards one another and thus begin to believe similar lies as well. Out of hurt, the daughters may decide that "all men are jerks," while sons will decide that "women aren't to be trusted". And so, we have an increase being passed on to the next generation.

As for my struggle with hugs, there was no apparent increase. Yet, if I had kept on thinking I was just a "non-hugger" and chose not to deal with it, an increase may have occurred. If I had children before dealing with this issue, I probably would have passed this lie on to them by the way I treated them or by neglecting to hug them.

As you consider a particular issue in your own life, ask yourself whether it exhibits any of the characteristics of reaping. If it does, then the good news is there is something that can begin to be done about it.

Things to Cultivate
- What are some of the issues in your life that appear to be bad fruit?
- One at a time, take each of the issues that appear as bad fruit, and answer the following questions:
    Fruit – What is being produced in my life that makes it apparent that this is bad fruit?
    Seasons – What are the particular times or conditions when the bad fruit occurs?
    Persistence – Does this fruit persist no matter what I have tried to do to stop it?
    Increase – Have I noticed an increase? Do my children show signs of being affected by my bad fruit?

RIPE

Sow for yourselves righteousness, reap the fruit of unfailing love,
and break up your unplowed ground;
for it is time to seek the LORD,
until he comes and showers righteousness on you.
But you have planted wickedness, you have reaped evil,
you have eaten the fruit of deception.
Hosea 10:12-13a.

Prepare your confession and come back to GOD.
Pray to him, 'Take away our sin, accept our confession.
Receive as restitution our repentant prayers."
Hosea 14:2 (MSG).

God wants us to deal with our bad fruit.

One Saturday morning while I was lying in bed, a word popped into my head. Some people get great ideas in the shower or when they're driving. Mine seem to come when I'm just waking up. Anyway, I believe God gave me this word to help in remembering the steps one needs to take to process the bad fruit in their life. It's the acronym **RIPE** which stands for:

- **R**ecognize – recognize the bad fruit
- **I**dentify--identify the root issues
- **P**ray through – pray through the root issues
- **E**xhibit – exhibit good fruit

Over the course of our lives different issues will surface, and as they do they become evident, or we might say "ripe." As we recognize the bad fruit ripening in our lives, we are at this point able to begin identifying what the root issues might be that go along with it. Unfortunately, for most of us this bad fruit has already ripened quite awhile ago, and despite our best efforts (or denial) it has gotten a bit rotten and smelly.

The good news is that once we are able to identify the root issues, we can really do something lasting about all that smelly stuff--by praying through it. This "praying through it" is what paves the way for the production of good fruit where once only bad existed.

The following chapters will provide you with an understanding of the four parts of **RIPE**: **R**ecognize, **I**dentify, **P**ray through, and **E**xhibit. Also, there are some helpful insights provided as to what bad fruit might look like and where you might find it. By gaining a better understanding about **RIPE**, you'll become equipped with the knowledge of exactly what to do when bad fruit becomes ripe in *your* life.

Recognize the Bad Fruit

By their fruit
you shall recognize them.
Matthew 7:16a

For this people's heart has become calloused;
they hardly hear with their ears, and they have closed their eyes.
Otherwise they might see with their eyes, hear with their ears,
understand with their hearts and turn, and I would heal them. But
blessed are your eyes because they see,
and your ears because they hear.
Matthew 13:15-16

God wants us to see our bad fruit and turn to Him so He may heal us.

Where we used to live, we had a very large backyard. Around the house, I put in a lawn that extended from the street all the way around the house and then halfway into the backyard. The rest I left as an open field where I didn't plant any grass. It was sort of like a meadow and made us feel like we lived out in the country. From time to time I would mow this field in order to keep the weeds under control. I did this all over except where there were these pretty patches of yellow flowering plants.

You see, to me these yellow flowering plants looked rather nice, and besides they gave color to the backyard. As far as I was concerned they were beautiful and harmless.

Then one day I was informed that these "beautiful" plants were actually a type of noxious weed called tansies. You can imagine my surprise! I then learned that they are categorized as noxious weeds because they choke out native grasses, decreasing the food supply for deer and other such animals. In addition, they're not native to the area, they have a bitter taste, and most animals will not eat them. Further, not only were they considered "noxious", but I discovered that I was bound by law to get rid of them!

Wow! So here I was actually cultivating noxious weeds (sowing). In addition I was hurting the natural grasses and plants while affecting the food supply for native animals (causing trouble). And lastly I was assisting in the developing and propagating of their seeds (reaping with an increase), not only in my yard but my neighbors' yards as well (defiling many), since the seeds where being spread about by the wind. This was all occurring right before my very eyes, and I didn't even realize the harm. Until then, I had never thought of doing anything about it since I never recognized those yellow flowering plants as a problem.

Perhaps the most important key in dealing with bad fruit is recognizing it for what it is. Though others can see and point out our problem areas to us, nothing can be done about them until *we* see and acknowledge them as a problem for ourselves.

Growing up, I was told I was such a good little boy. I never made waves--I did what I was told. I was told I had an "easy-going personality". That sounded good to me and I accepted it as the way God made me. Besides, I was often praised for being this way with such comments as,

Perhaps the most important key in dealing with bad fruit is a willingness to recognize it.

"What a nice young man you are," or "You are such a good boy."

The truth of the matter was that my "easy-going personality" was actually a "passive personality" in disguise, and hence bad fruit. But I had never considered it as bad fruit in my life until I got married.

This all came to light whenever my wife and I would get into arguments. My wife began to complain that she couldn't have a good fight with me because I was so passive. I would agree with every issue she brought up and always be the first to apologize. There was no strength in me for her to bounce her feelings off of. I couldn't identify with her or meet her in her frustrations, hurts and anger. Worse yet, my passive behavior actually made her feel judged for having the feelings she did have. Here I would be acting all calm, peaceful and apologetic in the midst of an "argument" where she was the only one losing her cool.

She felt alone and unprotected, even patronized. All this did was to exasperate her even more. Yet, at the time, I had no understanding of the problem I was creating. I just thought I was being a nice guy and she was somehow really upset.

Fortunately, one day God gave me some insight. This happened when I entertained the idea of, "Could this pattern in our arguments actually be bad fruit?" As I considered this I began to see that my passivity did not make my wife feel loved, for it was actually driving us apart. I soon began to realize that there were other areas in my life where there had been bad fruit concerning this same issue. I just had never seen it as such until now. And how could I. I had throughout my life identified "passive" as "easy-going", and who I was. And besides, I had been praised for it!

But thinking further about my childhood, I remembered how hard it had always been for me to stand up for myself. I got around this by learning how to avoid bullies and become the campus "nice guy." I would "let things go" when I should have asserted myself. I also struggled with taking initiative.

Now, being married, this character trait of passivity especially affected my wife. I thought I understood what taking initiative meant, but the practice of it often eluded me. I pretty much just floated through life, letting others make decisions for me. Often I mistook this as the Lord directing me.

I also realized I was motivated more by fear than by love. It often took the fear of someone getting angry with me to get me going. And I saw why she was so angry--she didn't want to be the one to have to motivate me and get me to do something. After all those years of growing up and

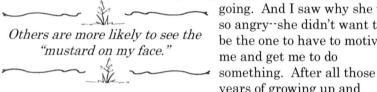

Others are more likely to see the "mustard on my face."

thinking I was just a "nice guy", I finally began to recognize some of my behavior as the bad fruit it actually was. Further, I came to see how this bad fruit was hurting and defiling those around me.

Once I was able to recognize my passivity as bad fruit, I was then ready to look for root causes. I soon discovered that my bad fruit was rooted in times when I had given-up, times when I felt my feelings hadn't mattered. I recalled a time I judged my father as a young boy during an argument he had had with my mother. I saw him lord his authority over her in a hurtful way, and thus made a decision to never be like him. There were also times when, as a child, my own anger was not acknowledged. I felt ignored and came to believe it didn't do any good to be angry.

Looking back, I realized that my mother didn't have time to deal with my feelings. She was raising three boys on her own, she had to work full-time and she was trying to recover from the brokenness of divorce. She is an amazing woman and I give her tremendous credit for all she did for us during those hard years. Yet, as a little boy I had judged her and my father at various times. And this caused me to bear the bad fruit of becoming passive.

As I began praying through these roots, the good fruit started to come. Some came right away. Some in other areas took awhile, as more and more memories surfaced and were prayed through.

As a result, I became more able to "meet" my wife—both in conversation and "heated discussion"! I began to understand her anger and frustration. And I came to discover my own! I became more of a friend to her and a much better sparring partner as well. Over time, we grew closer to each other, both of us feeling more heard and understood. I also started taking more initiative with things—making family decisions, working harder to provide, and setting limits with the kids. I grew to be motivated more by love than by fear. But again, the first key component that started this process was for me to be able to recognize something as the bad fruit that it really was.

Not identifying something as bad fruit happens for several reasons. One reason is because some people have not been informed that something is bad fruit. For others, they simply don't see something as bad fruit even when it

Circumstances and others merely reveal what is in me, revealing clues about my roots.

is pointed out to them. Some love their bad fruit, so why would they want to give it up? Yet others would rather choose denial since they don't believe that anything can be done about their bad fruit. And perhaps they have already tried all sorts of self-helps which didn't work and they are simply worn out.

I was on a picnic once when one of my friends looked at me and pointed out there was mustard on my face. Obviously, I couldn't see my own face or I would have known to take care of it myself. Sure enough when I wiped my face, I found he was right. Though I might have been a little embarrassed, I was glad my friend cared enough to point it out.

I have found that others are more likely to see the "mustard on my face" than I am--whether it is something I am ignoring or I am simply not aware of. Although their feedback at times may not be completely accurate, there is often a bit of truth in what they say. So if we are willing, it might be good to consider that there might be bad fruit that others are seeing that I just may not be able to see for myself. It takes humility to be able to receive what is being offered. Just ask God to show you how to separate the "meat" from the "bones."

Sometimes it's difficult to recognize the bad fruit in our lives because it's simply something we're not used to doing. We may be extremely skilled at finding it in others, but when it comes to ourselves we are sorely out of practice. For some reason it is human nature to want others to change first, or to change for our sake. We find it much more natural to put the blame on someone else and assume the victim role for ourselves. The problem with this is that it tends to make us feel that we can't experience freedom until someone (or something) else changes first. This unnecessarily puts us at their mercy, dependent upon their choices before we can experience relief.

Years ago, in seeking help for my conflicts with my wife, I met with a counselor friend of mine. He was very empathetic. He listened for quite some time to my side of the story. He seemed to know I needed to share my frustrations and to feel heard. In summary my complaints mostly revolved around, "If only my wife would only change, then ..."

Yet, at some point he knew that I needed to be confronted about my false assumption. And so he told me, "Your wife may never change" with a pause for effect. "There is only one person who can change, and that person is you." At this I felt panic--how could I go on if my wife never changed?!

But, I later realized how much I had an "others must change first" mentality. Plain and simple, I was being selfish and self-centered. So, I decided to begin following the advice given and work on myself— to do what was in my power to do. Yes, I did need to share my frustrations and hurts, but I also needed to focus on recognizing the bad fruit in my life. I can't change others but I can change myself by dealing with the root issues in my own life. Consequently, if others never changed, at least I would be able to remove the things in my heart that made me vulnerable to being hurt by others.

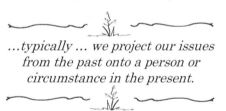

...typically ... we project our issues from the past onto a person or circumstance in the present.

Is your peace and sense of well-being dependent upon others or on circumstances? Does it change as they change? Perhaps you never considered this as bad fruit. I know for me that my peace used to seem so often directly related to my relationship with my wife.

Sure enough, when I began to work more on my stuff and focus less on my wife, it did make a difference. And, over time our relationship has definitely gotten better--my peace is more inwardly driven. Not only have I been blessed by the change in me, but so has my wife.

What typically happens in a problematic relationship is that we project our issues from the past onto a person or circumstance in the

Pray Through It

present. We don't do this intentionally. It is something our heart seems to do automatically out of reaction to the unresolved root issues in our heart. Why? Because *this* person who just irritated me is tangible; they are in the present. What this person has done is to remind my heart of a familiar feeling from my past. But because I am not in touch with my past-related problem, my heart overreacts by putting the blame for what I feel on the person whose actions reminded my heart in the first place.

If you recall as I shared earlier, there was a man who projected his unresolved father issues onto me by getting into an argument with me. Because I was an authority figure, and we quarreled, that is all it took for him

Sometimes we are unable to identify bad fruit because other issues are more pressing.

to feel his past pain. Yet, at no time did he consciously feel it had anything to do with his father. It seemed to him to be all about me, and he continued to feel that way until I did something his father had never done before, by letting him win and showing him our relationship was more important. This freed his heart up to start seeing the bad fruit for what it was and then connect it to the correct root cause in his past..

Sometimes, we are unable to identify bad fruit because other issues are more pressing. I had a professor in college who, while on a train in India, got a chance to chat with a government official. Being interested in different cultures, he asked the official what were some of the typical psychological issues people in India dealt with. The official just stared at him saying nothing, as if he did not understand the question. So, he asked again. Again, the man looked at the professor as if astonished that he would ask such a question. Finally, the man replied by saying that most people in India are probably not concerned about or even aware of such issues. Most people in India were more concerned about basic things like where they'd be getting their next meal from. Basic survival was more important--they did not have the luxury of dwelling on their psychological needs.

Perhaps most of us can't relate to the threat of starvation, but we can relate to just trying to survive on a day by day basis. I have known many people who are so consumed by legal issues, finances, or divorce proceedings that they can't stop to see how their bad fruit might play into what they are facing. At the moment, all their energy and time is being focused on other pending matters.

But, if we *are* freed up enough so as to be able to identify bad fruit in our lives, we shouldn't be discouraged when it's being brought to our attention. We need to see it as God moving to set us free, so we can do our part to fulfill His plan for our lives. Chances are, the very thing that's irritating us right now might be the very thing He is trying to get us to recognize as bad fruit. It also might be the very thing that is holding us back in some way until it is prayed through.

Things to Cultivate
- Have there been some issues in your life that you now see as bad fruit which you originally didn't recognize as such?
- What kept you from seeing it for what it was?
- In what ways have you wanted others to change in order to make you happier or make your life run smoother? Now, try taking these things to the Lord. Confess any selfishness on your part. Ask Him to help you see what your contribution is to the problem. Ask Him for the courage to work on yourself and your own bad fruit first.

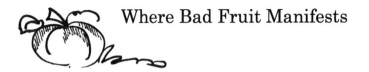

Where Bad Fruit Manifests

Even as I have seen, they that plow iniquity,
and sow wickedness, reap the same.
Job 4:8 (KJV)

God made it simple for us - -What we sow will become evident in our lives through what we reap.

I thought it would be beneficial to provide some examples of bad fruit, illustrating areas where it often manifests. To assist in this, I have divided these areas into three basic groupings: bad fruit which manifests in relation to ourselves, in relation to others, and in relation to our circumstances. As you read through the next three sections of this book, you will be able to get some idea of what bad fruit may look like and where it may be manifesting in your life. You might even find it showing up in ways you hadn't noticed before. As you do, I would encourage you to share what you have discovered with someone you know and trust, especially if they, too, understand the principles of sowing and reaping. By sharing your observations out loud you will gain more insight and see more clearly the bad fruit in your life. Another idea is to journal about what you have come to discover.

Fruit Inspection

The following is an exercise that you might find to be very helpful. It will assist you in determining and clarifying if something you suspect as bad fruit is bad fruit or not. So, be sure to take your time on this part.

Get a piece of paper and create four columns. Then write on the paper as follows:

Fruit Inspection			
Bad Fruit	Seasons	Persists	Increase

As you recognize a specific manifestation of bad fruit in your life, enter it in the first column. Then, fill in each column accordingly for each type of bad fruit you list. Let's use my bad fruit concerning hugs as an example. Under the first column I would write: "Difficulty giving and receiving hugs." In the second column, I would write: "Whenever I am in places where people give hugs." In the third column, I would write: "It persists though I put effort out to give and receive hugs. I still feel awkward, uncomfortable and mechanical." And in the last column I would write: "No." Though my responses are short, you should feel free to write as much as you need to express your experiences. And, don't forget to ask the Lord for insight as you do this.

In going through this exercise, you may sometimes find that what you thought was bad fruit really isn't. Just because a person has a bad day four times in one week doesn't necessarily mean they are experiencing bad fruit. Remember, we are looking for specific patterns that indicate there is a deeper root cause to the problem.

Bad Fruit Manifesting in Ourselves

For out of the abundance of the heart his mouth speaks.
Luke 6:45b (NKJV)

God designed our hearts to give us clues, through what we express, as to what is hidden inside, both good and bad. While reading this next chapter, you may see some similarities between the examples given and your own experiences. If so, don't be overly concerned, this does not *necessarily* mean it is bad fruit in your life. Keep in mind the characteristics of bad fruit: it is fruitful, persistent, seasonal and increasing. Use these characteristics as your guide.

When I speak of bad fruit manifesting in "ourselves", I am referring to bad fruit showing up in how we see ourselves, which is often expressed in how we behave and think. We might in our minds believe one thing to be true about ourselves, but at the same time struggle with believing it in our hearts.

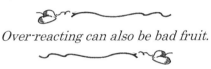

Over-reacting can also be bad fruit.

Perhaps we struggle with negative thoughts despite what we know to be true. Perhaps we battle with being overly critical toward ourselves. Often, these thoughts feel familiar yet are still uncomfortable and hurtful, and are associated with feelings that are debilitating or interfere with what we need to get done. It may seem that we struggle in an endless fight to resist these thoughts and keep them down. For some, there is no longer any fight, and they have simply come to believe the lies that they are "stupid" and "unloved".

For others, the issue may be around the desire to punish themselves to keep from doing "that stupid thing" again. There might be a pattern of self-sabotage (like never being able to finish anything) along with the fear of failure, or even of success. They may find themselves saying things like, "I can't do anything right," or "I'll never amount to anything." Out of defeat, they may have decided, "This is just the way I am."

Over-reacting can also be a type of bad fruit. "Reacting" is often appropriate whereas over-reacting is not. As I like to say, "The overage in the reacting is usually coming from a different source." So, no matter how justified our *reaction* is, we need to own and take responsibility for the "over" part.

And where does the "over" part of over-reacting come from? If this is a pattern in our lives (and not just because we didn't get our coffee this morning), generally the present event is reminding our hearts of something similar we experienced in the past. So, the overage comes generally comes from an unresolved issue hidden there. "For out of the abundance of the heart his mouth speaks." (Luke 6:45b, NKJV) Therefore, what's in my heart will come out eventually, both the good and the bad.

Bad fruit often shows up in the realm of our feelings.

The opposite is just as true, where "under"-reacting is the bad fruit. We may have become a person who withdraws or acts passively as a defense mechanism in order to avoid conflict or revealing our true selves. When this is bad fruit, it is often rooted in times when we were made to feel defeated and our hearts came to believe that nothing we could say or do would matter. This is where the lies of, "What good will it do?!", "Nobody listens to me anyway," and, "No one cares how I feel" come from.

Bad fruit also shows up in the realm of our feelings. This might be seen in one's inability to cry, empathize or grieve. Some of us may not be able to feel or recognize certain emotions. It is as if we have shut them off and we are disconnected from them. But, the fact of the matter is, though we may have gone numb to our feelings, we still have them even if we don't realize it.

In reality, there's no such thing as an unexpressed feeling. If it doesn't come out the way it should, it will come out "sideways" in ways it was not intended to be expressed. And, when it does come out in this manner, it doesn't bring relief. Frequently, this is through persistent and re-occurring physical problems, such as headaches, feelings

...there's no such thing as an unexpressed feeling.

of depression, ulcers, neck and back pains, sleep disturbances, and frequent illnesses. This is not to say that every headache or other physical ailment points to a stuffed emotion. But rather, when we do stuff our emotions these symptoms can be evidence of that.

While growing up, how many of us heard, "Big boys (or girls) don't cry" or, "If you don't stop crying, I'll give you something to cry about!" You see, if we grew up hearing such things as a child, and then held hidden resentment in our hearts about it, we will now find that the tears don't come, even when something happens which would normally justify a good cry. Are we uncomfortable when others cry, or are we sympathetic? Do we find ourselves wanting to shut down our tears or even the tears of others? Do we view the expression of feelings as weakness?

Judgments we have made about our feelings can keep us from being able to grieve properly. Grief is something you have to go *through,* not around. The bad fruit of stuffing our feelings can either be the inability to grieve or simply the inability to prevent getting stuck in the grief process. This is because it is necessary to acknowledge and express the gamut of feelings as they come to the surface while grieving.

As for me, over a period of time I began to recognize different ways I had the bad fruit of stuffing my feelings. As I worked through these, a very interesting thing happened. You see, for years whenever I had a runny nose from a cold, flu or allergy, I would routinely get a sinus infection as well. These were

Grief is something you have to go through, not around.

frequently painful and just made things drag on a lot longer than they should have. But, one day I noticed that the sinus infections were becoming less frequent, to the point where I rarely got one. Looking back, it was as if my sinus infections were a symptom of all my stuffed tears and feelings over the years. So, not only did I get my ability to acknowledge my feelings back, I also got rid of my susceptibility to sinus infections.*

Addictions, too, are very often the outcome of an attempt to stuff or numb the pain of unresolved past issues. They are in essence a symptom of bad fruit. The bad fruit is the persistent enticement towards some sort of addiction in order to make the feelings, which emanate from the root issues, go away.

Addictions are very often an attempt to stuff or avoid feeling the pain of unresolved past issues.

As we all know, it is quite unsettling to have a negative feeling that keeps surfacing, without knowing exactly where it's coming from. This is especially true when it won't seem to go away—despite denial, blame shifting, drinking, etc. Often, it is the *feeling* portion of a memory that our heart recalls first. And, being that it's painful, we want to run from it in order to avoid the hurt and the

---

* It is important to note that having repetitive sinus infections does not mean that one has root issues around stuffing their feelings. Though this might be a possibility, one should avoid making such generalities as in certain symptoms indicate a specific root problem. Instead, each apparent bad fruit issue needs to be considered for the uniqueness of its own.

recollection of the incidents from whence it originates. The use of alcohol, or drugs, or pornography is simply one way to "numb" the discomfort, by providing a pleasing yet temporary distraction from the pain.

What I have noticed is that most of us tend to gravitate towards something that "works" for us, that is, something that we find effective at distracting us from our negative feelings. Now you might say, "What are talking about? I don't have any addictions." Most of us, when we hear the word "addiction" think of such things as gambling, alcoholism, pornography, the taking of illegal drugs or over use of pain medications. What we don't realize is that addictions are determined by *what they do for us*, not a list of specific activities or things.

With this understanding, our list of addictions should actually be much larger than is commonly recognized. Our list should, in fact, include (but not be limited to) such things as food, work-alcoholism, television, hobbies, caffeine (coffee, chocolate, etc.), video games, the Internet, cleaning, shopping, romance novels, etc. Many of these things are not wrong in and of themselves. But, what we need to ask ourselves is, "Why are we hooked on them?"

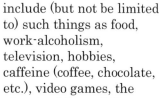

...most of us tend to gravitate towards something that "works" for us...

Television was one of the things that "worked" for me. I used to watch inordinate amounts of TV. I liked TV, it distracted me. It numbed the discomfort I felt from all sorts of root issues. The bad fruit was my inability to deal with my feelings. The symptom was my addiction to television.

Chocolate was another one of my addictions. Without realizing it, I was using it to deal with my stuffed feelings concerning anger. I just thought I loved eating chocolate. It wasn't until I got my ability to feel anger back that I realized the connection. For when I got it back, I lost my *addiction* to chocolate. I noticed that I no longer had to eat dozens of chocolate chip cookies before becoming satiated. By recognizing my inability to get angry as bad fruit, and then dealing with it, my addiction went away.

Since television and chocolate "worked" for me in numbing my feelings and avoiding issues, I'm now more in tune to my desires for them. They are familiar. I recognize the feelings that draw me to them. Whenever I find myself wanting to consume large amounts of chocolate, I try to stop and ask myself, "Am I trying to avoid some stuffed feelings or an unresolved issue?" Likewise, whenever I am drawn to watch episode after episode of a sci-fi show I like, I try to pause and look a little deeper. I try to ask the Lord if there is anything I'm avoiding.

By the way, I still love chocolate. I even have a coffee mug that someone gave me which says, "Life, liberty and the pursuit of chocolate!" And, it's okay for me to still love it. What has changed is the power which chocolate, and TV, have in enticing me to avoid certain problems in my life.

So, stuffing and avoiding our feelings is often bad fruit, but inappropriately expressing them might be bad fruit as well. We should not deny or ignore how we feel. We need to at least acknowledge our feelings for what they are. And, we need to do whatever is appropriate in order to process them. But, this does not mean it's okay to do whatever we feel, to let ourselves get out of control, or to sin. We are each responsible for our actions regardless of how we may feel

Perhaps we are not able to get angry or, when we do, we over-react. Whether we implode or explode, we need to consider that either extreme could, for us, be bad fruit. Are we uncomfortable with our feelings? Do we avoid situations which require us to share how we feel? Do we draw shame or guilt to ourselves, as if we were some sort of magnet? Or, do we "over"-sympathize

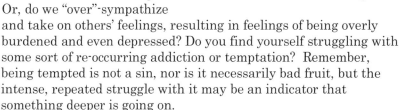

Being tempted is not a sin, nor is it necessarily bad fruit.

and take on others' feelings, resulting in feelings of being overly burdened and even depressed? Do you find yourself struggling with some sort of re-occurring addiction or temptation? Remember, being tempted is not a sin, nor is it necessarily bad fruit, but the intense, repeated struggle with it may be an indicator that something deeper is going on.

One day, I was out with my daughter shopping for a gift for my wife. While I was in this one shop, I looked across the store and noticed a woman with long blond hair. She had her back to me so I couldn't see her face. Now, there is nothing wrong with noticing someone or seeing that they are attractive. But, what I felt was this inclination or "pull" to go to that part of the store, with the seemingly innocent purpose of seeing "what's over there." It was a mere curiosity; that's all. But isn't that how all temptations initially start? I recognized the "pull" as inappropriate and the rationale as a temptation. So, I did the wise thing and left.

Even after I had pulled away in my car, I could still feel the "pull", though it had lessened some. Knowing what I do now about bad fruit, I decided it would be a good idea to look deeper and attempt to figure out why this feeling wasn't leaving me. What I have learned, is that behind most temptations is an inappropriate attempt to fulfill an appropriate need. So, I thought to myself, "What appropriate need does my heart think would be fulfilled if I were to entertain the temptation I was having while in the store?" As I pondered legitimate, God-given, needs such as receiving affirmation, being heard, feeling understood, being comforted, having a friend, etc., the need for comfort seemed to stand out. I asked the Lord, "When did I need comfort but didn't get it?" And, He began to show me times when, as a child, I needed comfort but didn't get it. I then prayed through those experiences as they came to mind and an amazing thing happened--the "pull" went away.

The above are just a few ways that bad fruit shows up in relation to our own selves. Perhaps you have thought of some others on your own. The first step in any healing process is recognizing that there's even a problem. If you're starting to see some bad fruit in your own life, you've already taken that first step!

Things to Cultivate

- In what ways do you over-react?
- In what ways do you under-react?
- What types of things "work" for you (addictions) in an attempt to avoid discomfort and negative feelings?
- What types of temptations seem to be very persistent and difficult in resisting? What do you think is the appropriate need your heart is trying to fill in an inappropriate way?
- In what other ways do you see bad fruit manifesting in yourself? Perhaps you have thought of an example that was not given.

Bad Fruit Manifesting in Relation to Others

A friend loves at all times,
And a brother is born for adversity.
Proverbs 17:17 (NASB)

Faithful are the wounds of a friend,
But deceitful are the kisses of an enemy.
Proverbs 27:6 (NASB)

God often allows our interactions with others to reveal what is really in us.

As you read along, you may again be able to relate to several of the examples given. But, as before, keep in mind that bad fruit has the characteristics of being fruitful, seasonal, persistent and increasing. Therefore, though you may see similarities between the following examples and the interpersonal relationships in your life, do not be too quick to assume they are necessarily bad fruit.

When bad fruit shows up in our relationships with others, it's usually in how we react to things they say or do. It may also

Negative expectations most often get written upon our hearts because of judgments we made about past experiences.

manifest in how they interact or don't interact with us.

Perhaps we seem to somehow attract certain kinds of people who bring out the worst in us, who take advantage of us, or who put us down and reject us. We find ourselves saying, "Why do men (or women) always treat me that way?", "Why do people always take advantage of me?", or "Why is it always the losers who are attracted to me?" This is reaping bad fruit in relationships.

Some of us have gotten hurt and disappointed so many times that we've given up when it comes to relationships. We've lowered our expectations and believed lies such as, "That's just the way men (or women) are." Where the truth of the matter is that that is just the *type* of men (or women) we attract and/or to whom we are attracted. As much as we may hate it, we feel doomed to swim and fish in a pond full of less than optimal candidates.

Perhaps our bad fruit shows up in our relationship with our spouse. We were, and are, attracted to our spouse for lots of reasons. We desire a close relationship, to love someone and to be loved. In many ways they seem to fulfill some of our desires. Yet in some areas, this other person may actually fulfill our negative expectations, those coming from root issues. We wake up one day and say, "This is *not* the person I thought I married." Some even wake up saying, "Oh no. I married my mother!"

Negative expectations are often bad fruit. Because of past experiences in relationships we may have made a generalization in our heart such as, "All men are . . ." or, "All women are. . ." And so, to our surprise (and for some it's not a surprise) we experience some of these same things in on-going relationships, especially if we are married. This occurs despite our efforts to not become, or marry, someone like we had judged.

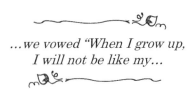

...we vowed "When I grow up, I will not be like my...

We may see bad fruit in relation to our children. Perhaps we are too harsh with them—or too lenient. We may show favoritism, or be so afraid to show it that we lean too far in the other direction. Perhaps we are uncomfortable playing or relating to our children. Do we do things out of love or guilt for our children? Are we overcompensating for a need that didn't get filled in our lives? Do we feel easily manipulated and out of control? Do our children seem to bring the worst out of us? This "worst" is often a symptom of our bad fruit. Where we feel easily manipulated by our children, we need to ask ourselves if we judged our parents for the way they treated others (or us) and are therefore over-compensating out of fear of repeating their behavior.

To our dismay, some of us have discovered that we *have* become just like Mom or Dad. Or, we are the exact opposite, and have found that's not very effective either. How did this happen? It is likely that in the past we vowed, "When I grow up, I'll never be like my father (or mother)." Now, there may be some wisdom in not duplicating some of what our parents have done. But, if we make that decision out of resentment, we end up reaping bad fruit from it.

When someone says, concerning a son or daughter, "We don't get along because we are too much alike," I ask, "Then what is it that you don't like about yourself?" You see, if we liked everything about ourselves then we would enjoy those same things in our child.

Perhaps we get into arguments easily with people who possess certain personality traits. Maybe we are quick to feel belittled, powerless or non-existent around others. All it takes is for someone to say a simple little thing, like "That was *stupid*," or "I don't care," or "Women!" And if there is a certain tone that goes with it, all the worse! Certain people may make us feel controlled, guilty and ashamed. When this happens, do we find it takes an unusual amount of time to recover from the hurt? In some cases, we have to put out a tremendous effort to resist over-reacting to certain people's behaviors. Later, we rehearse imaginary arguments over and over again with the person who triggered us. And, of course, we win every time! But, when we are back in that person's presence, all our amazing arguments seem to vaporize. Our minds turn to mush. We can't think straight, and we say things we wish we hadn't. Then, all we want to do is run and hide.

Perhaps ... our identity comes from what we can do—not who we are.

Perhaps another's mood sets us off or seems to oppress us without a word even being spoken. Sometimes just a look, a smile, a smirk, or a laugh can stir up deep negative feelings within us. It could be a gesture like a raised hand, a pounding fist, something being hit or thrown, or someone turning away. Or, it could be someone crying or whining that overly annoys us. All these can bring up bad feelings and surface old but familiar lies like how "bad" think we are, how something is "always our fault", that we are responsible to "fix" things, or that we are "invisible".

Enabling is when we take on responsibility for another's feelings, life, or behavior. Feeling responsible in this manner is bad fruit. Have you found yourself rescuing people only to see them fall down again? Do you keep getting "burned" in relationships? Do you excuse someone's sinful behavior with such thoughts as "They can't help it", "That's just the way they are" or "Who would help them if I didn't?" Do you always seem to attract people who take advantage of you? If so, you may need to ask yourself when the first time was that you took on responsibility that wasn't yours.

In other instances, we may have felt obligated to take care of a parent emotionally. We may have felt responsible for their feelings. Perhaps they even made us feel guilty for all the "pain" we caused them. Thus, as an adult, we find we are motivated by guilt and obligation, not love. Perhaps we were validated only for our abilities, so we find our identity in what we do—not who we are.

Bad fruit in relation to others may also come according to what another represents to us, such as an authority figure. Maybe our boss seems to always overlook us when it comes to recognition or getting a raise. Maybe we get blamed for everything that goes wrong at work. It seems that no matter how great we are on the job, we continue to reap supervisors who are cranky and demanding and who, come to think about it, remind us an awful lot of Dad!

God represents, and is, many things to us, especially when it comes to our needs. So, it is easy to see why we often project our unhealed authority issues at the Lord. For instance, when someone calls into question God's supposed lack of care ("How could a loving God let so much suffering happen?"), this is often evidence of resentments against earlier caregivers. Perhaps there was neglect. Maybe there were terrible things that happened and no one did anything to stop it. When such is the case, I ask, "So what was it like growing up? Were you loved? Were you neglected? Were things done fairly?" This often reveals the true source of their issues with God.

Do you experience a conflict between what you know to be true about God and what your heart feels? Do you have selective hearing in that you hear His commands but not His words of affirmation?

God is so secure, that even though we may project our issues onto Him, He continues to love us anyway. He knows well the place from whence our hurt originates and isn't offended when we mistakenly think it is about Him. God is big enough and loving enough to let us express how we feel about Him, even when it's not true. We see this many times over in the Psalms. He is very willing to be a sounding board, to let us get the hurts and lies out where we can see them. My only advice is that, once you do, you move to take the next step. Ask Him where those feelings came from and when you first started to feel that way. . .

Things to Cultivate

- What types of people consistently seem to be able to make you feel hurt, rejected or inappropriately angry?
- What types of words, phrases or looks are able to make you over-react, feel bad or withdraw?
- Are there anything about God, Himself, you struggle with? If so, what is it?
- In what other ways do you see bad fruit manifesting in your relationships with others? Perhaps you have thought of an example that was not given.

Bad Fruit Manifesting in Our Circumstances

I have learned to be content in all circumstances.
Philippians 4:11a-13 (NIV)

God often uses the circumstances in our lives to reveal what is in us.

As before, while reading through the examples provided, be sure to keep in mind the characteristics of bad fruit—that it is fruitful, seasonal, persistent and increasing. Since you might relate to several of the examples given, this will help you identify those that are more likely to be bad fruit and those that are not.

Is your peace dependent upon circumstances? Do you have to have things "just so" in order to feel peace? Do you live in constant worry about the future, making it difficult to enjoy the present because of incessant worries about money or health? Is your mind cluttered with "What if..." questions? Are you tormented with regrets? Or, do you live in the past, at the expense of the present, because of the inability to resolve those regrets?

When it comes to bad fruit in our circumstances and life, I often refer to this pattern as "phenomena-logical." This is when there are certain events or phenomena which persist in our lives despite our efforts to minimize or prevent them. They seem to happen on their own, and more frequently to us than to others. We feel that in these areas we are the exception to the basic rules of life—that we're somehow different from most other people.

In the area of finances, the bad fruit might be that no matter how consistent we are at tithing and budgeting, we never seem to get ahead. When we work harder, it doesn't seem to make any difference. We never seem to have enough. Something seems to keep "stealing" our money-- things are always breaking down or we have continual unforeseen emergencies. If one or more of these experiences describe you, try asking yourself these questions: "While growing up, did I feel that money was more important to my parents than I was?" "Was money the main theme of my parents' arguments?" "Did someone frequently say, 'We don't have any money for that,' when what really happened was that it got spent on drugs or alcohol?"

Bad fruit can show up in our work and in what we do. We may seem to get jobs that never quite fit who we are. Maybe our co-workers get away with things while we are singled out for every

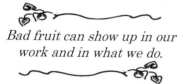

Bad fruit can show up in our work and in what we do.

mistake we make. Or, maybe we repeatedly get into jobs where we get laid off or where the work is too stressful.

Our possessions too may give evidence of bad fruit. Some people always seem buy things that break down. One man I met owned a great deal and yet he couldn't bring himself to enjoy it. Do we find ourselves looking to the next purchase to make us happy? Do we tend to be given gifts which suggest that "no one really knows" us?

Bad fruit may be evident with our time, like that we are always late, or we resent those who are. Maybe we frequently lose track of the time and life is a constant blur. Maybe we have trouble resting in the moment, or find we're always looking toward tomorrow. For some, it is like their time just gets consumed or there never seems to be enough of it. Are we able to project hope into the future? Are we tied to the past, unable to move forward? Are we stuck in grief? When it comes to making a decision or getting something done, do we always wait until the last minute? Or worse, are we unable to make a decision until we are forced to do so? Maybe we consistently forget certain birthdays or events and are usually buying gifts at the last minute.

Again, just because we are experiencing difficult times doesn't necessarily mean there is a root cause in our past. It's when life seems to be way out of balance, and consistently so, that we need to take heed. When we seem to have more than our share of problems and they

Bad fruit may be evident with our time...

do not resolve over time--when we find ourselves saying things like, "Life is unfair", "Why does this always happen to me?" or "Nothing I do seems to make any difference..." we can be pretty sure we are dealing with some root issues. If you have patterns like this in your life they just might be bad fruit.

You see, life *is* unfair and hard sometimes, but life is also fun and good. And life is even enjoyable! The truth is that life is multi-faceted. But, when we judge it for its difficulties and make emphatic negative statements about it, this seems to invite even more of the same. As a result, this shuts down our ability to enjoy

Pray Through It

the other aspects of life. When we recognize this, we need to ask ourselves, "Where in my past did I decide these things about life?"

"Life is ..." statements are a common response to difficult times, and they may represent exactly how we feel. Yet, when such a statement is accompanied by sin (bitterness, resentment, and unforgiveness) and not prayed through, it begins to make life seem hateful.

Whether our bad fruit manifests in ourselves, others or circumstances, the most important part is recognizing it as bad fruit. Once this has been done we are then ready to go in search of the root cause.

Things to Cultivate

- Is there an aspect of life which you consider particularly difficult?
- Is there a phenomenon in your life that occurs concerning finances? If so, what?
- Is there a phenomenon in your life that occurs concerning time? If so, what?
- Complete the following sentence in the context of how you see your life, "Whenever _____happens, then _____happens."
- In what other ways do you see bad fruit manifesting in your circumstances? Perhaps you have thought of an example that was not given.

Identifying Root Issues

Investigate my life, O God, find out everything about me; Cross-examine and test me, get a clear picture of what I'm about; See for yourself whether I've done anything wrong-- then guide me on the road to eternal life.
Psalms 139:23-24 (MSG)

God knows everything about us.

Whenever we begin attempting to identify root issues, we should always be sure to invite Him into the process. Who better knows our past, and who better knows what events in our past are connected to the bad fruit we are battling in the present. Since He knows each of our lives from the beginning, I highly recommend seeking His guidance during the cross-examination process. Ask Him to help you recall those times from the past that follow the same theme as your bad fruit. Remember, once you have identified the theme behind your bad fruit, you will know where to start looking, as your root issues will follow that same theme.

Often, we can discover many root issues just by examining what we already know about our past. With the theme of your bad fruit in mind, ask yourself, "When else did I feel this way?" or, "When else did something like this happen?" For instance, if we feel that others like us only for what we *do*, we should ask ourselves something like, "When else didn't I feel accepted and loved just for who I am?"

Asking a friend to help in uncovering the root issues is very helpful. Often, having someone to listen as we share our thoughts helps us to remember things we haven't contemplated in a long time. Let the person you choose know that you'd like them to ask questions and reflect your thoughts back to you. Hopefully, they'll also give you some measure of understanding and affirmation, and be there to pray with you as old hurts surface.

When you feel that you have recalled as much as you can, go one step further and ask God to show you what you may have forgotten. This is helpful when nothing comes to mind at first that seems in sync with your bad fruit. Remember, He knows all things. He's been there all along. He remembers the times of trouble with much more clarity than you ever could. In fact, if you take the time to look back and listen to what the Lord has to say, you might be very surprised at what He will reveal.

For example, let's say that you have determined the theme of your bad fruit is something like, "I'm not good enough". With this in mind, you'd ask God, "When else did I feel like I wasn't good enough?" Then, just wait and listen to see what the Lord brings to mind.

As memories surface, write them down. Sometimes, one negative experience might be all there is behind the bad fruit you are dealing with. But, usually there are more. Where there is more than one, you need to realize that each memory on the same theme has, in its own way, served to reinforce the lies planted in your heart.

...once resentment sets in it is quite common to see it grow deeper and deeper ...

The way it generally works, is that when the first hurtful event happens we may not move straight to feelings of resentment. Perhaps we believe the best of someone, or quickly forgive them, or it "really doesn't seem to matter much." But, as hurts continue and multiply, we often grow weary of shrugging it off. And, after multiple insults, we finally come to the point of resenting the one who hurt us. Once resentment sets in, it is quite common to see it grow deeper and deeper with each successive offense, adding to the strength of the bad fruit in our present. Consequently, it is important to make a list detailing each memory along the same theme so each of them can be prayed through. It takes time—but it's worth it!

If possible, you might ask family members what they recall about your childhood and what the family dynamics were like from their point of view. Sometimes they can fill in gaps or jog your memory.

...it is from your perspective that you made judgments ...

Keep in mind that each person's perspective is different, but there might be some helpful information they can share. What matters is *your* perspective.

Perhaps, at the time of a particular memory, you saw things differently than others. That's okay—because it was from *your* perspective that you made judgments, and it is from those judgments that bad fruit came.

First, recall the important details. In other words, what happened? What was the story? Then, remember how it made you feel. What were you feeling at the time? Or, if you can't remember, how do you *think* you were feeling? Next, what was your sinful response to those who hurt you? And lastly, identify any lies you may have believed as a result of what happened. After a while, you will find that it'll become second nature to process memories in this way, and you'll get quicker at it.

Now, what do you do if you truly don't find any memories that fit? There might be several reasons for this, so don't be discouraged. In some cases, you might need to spend additional time clarifying the distinct features of the bad fruit. This can help you be more accurate when looking for your root issues. If you don't have the bad fruit correctly identified, it will be difficult to uncover the roots.

Often, the intensity of the search gets wearying, and the best thing to do is just leave it for awhile and go about your day as usual—you can always come back to it later. I have had root issues be identified within minutes of recognizing bad fruit. And then, I have had those that took weeks. There have even been some root issues that took months to uncover. Not to worry if this is the case with you, the timing may not be right. You might not be ready to face what you're afraid you'll find. The truth is, God can always be trusted. He knows when you're ready. He's not in a hurry. The thing to do is stay soft in His hands. Keep your ears and your heart open.

Often God wants us to ... to know we are loved even though we are not perfect...

Know that He loves you all along the journey, and that it's okay to be "a work in progress".

One other thing to consider is that perhaps you're not dealing with bad fruit at all. Your struggle may be coming from another source—you may just be battling rotten circumstances or the consequences of unwise choices.

What if the details of your past are sketchy though they fit the bad fruit? Or, what if all you know is a story you were told, but you don't actually remember it for yourself? Again, this is the time to ask the Lord for help with the details. Ask Him lots of questions, and then listen for the answers. If you still don't get any more insight but what you do have fits the pattern, run with it. Trust that you know all you need to and that God will make up the difference.

Again, keep in mind that not every difficult issue in life is due to unresolved past hurts. Perhaps, what we are in need of is medical attention. Perhaps, we lack self control or discipline. Maybe we are in burn-out or are sleep-deprived. Our diet may be unhealthy, we may need exercise. There is very real and practical help for all these things.

What I have come to realize is that I don't fully understand myself. I don't know the inner workings of my heart. What I do know, is that the One who created me knows how my heart works and how best to deal with it. As a result, I have made an open-ended prayer to the Lord. It is an on-going invitation for Him to search my heart and reveal to me what needs to be addressed. Therefore, when I see bad fruit manifesting in my life, and He points it out, I know I shouldn't be surprised. For when we give Him permission to change us, He often does just that.

In the Amplified Bible, Psalm 139:23-24 is just such an invitation. It says, "Search me [thoroughly], O God, and know my heart! Try me and know my thoughts! And see if there is any wicked *or* hurtful way in me, and lead me in the way everlasting."

This prayer is an invitation asking the Lord to take inventory of our hearts. And, Who better to "try and know" us—to reveal both the good and the bad fruit. Who better to show us "any wicked or hurtful way[s]", such as root issues. Who better to lead us to deal with them that we may walk in the way everlasting.

Things to Cultivate

When identifying your root issues, ask yourself these questions about the bad fruit:

- When else did I feel this way? When else did something similar happen?
- How did it make me feel?
- What was my sinful response to those involved?
- What lies and/or negative decisions did I make?

Digging for Roots

The following is an exercise that you might find to be very helpful. It will assist you in identifying and clarifying root issues. Be sure to take your time when doing this.

Get a piece of paper and create four columns. Then, write on your paper the following:

Digging for Roots	Bad Fruit: _____		
Instances	Feelings	My Response	Lies Believed

In illustrating how to fill in the chart, let's use the example of Shawn at the beginning of the book. One of his bad fruits was "feeling like I'm not good enough"--this is what would be written at the top as the bad fruit theme. The first column would say: "the time when dad was very late to my birthday party and could have been there but was out working". The second column would say: "not important", "rejected", "like I don't matter", "like he'd rather be some other place than with me". In the "Response" column would be: "I resented him". And in the "Lies" column would be: "I'm not good enough". Then this would be done again for each similar root issue. This is just an example, so you may want to elaborate more than this for each instance.

One other thing I would encourage you to do, is to write next to each lie what you know the truth to be. For instance, if one lie was: "I'm not good enough", the truth you could write would be: "I am lovable no matter what I can or cannot do," or perhaps, "I do many things well." If you aren't exactly sure what the truth is, ask a friend. And more importantly, ask the Lord—He'll tell you how He sees it from His point of view.

Pray Through It

If we confess our sins,
He is faithful and just to forgive us our sins,
and to cleanse us from all unrighteousness.
1 John 1:9 (KJV)

God provided a solution for our root issues and wants us to know it, so we can be set free from bearing bad fruit.

So, how do we put an end to the negative reaping in our lives? Now that we have recognized the bad fruit and have identified a number of root issues, what do we do next? Though it is helpful to know the origin of our struggles this knowledge alone is not enough to make their influence go away.

As shared earlier, it was our sinful response to a hurtful situation that became a seed planted in our lives which created an unresolved root issue and thus brought about bad fruit. Therefore, the solution must be a means to effectively remove what started the whole thing. It was not what happened to us or our circumstances that started it. It was not our feelings, even though we may have been tremendously hurt. And, it was not even those who hurt us, though their actions (or lack thereof) may have affected us very deeply. It was our *sinful response* to what happened that started it all. So, this is what needs to be addressed.

In the first few words of I John 1:9 it states what our part is—to confess our sins. When it comes to the sowing and reaping of bad fruit, our sins were our sinful responses to past situations. That sinful response was our unforgiveness towards those who we believed hurt us. And, our unforgiveness was

...He removes from our hearts our lingering sinful responses...

expressed in the form of such things as bitterness, resentment, judgments, hatred, revenge, etc. Therefore, our part is to confess that sinful response which started the process of sowing and reaping.

The rest of I John 1:9 is the Lord's part--it is His promised response to us when we do confess our sins. First of all, He promises to forgive us our sins, and secondly, He promises to cleanse us from all unrighteousness. Though it was the sowing of our sinful responses that started the reaping, it is His forgiveness that has the power to uproot it. It is God, Himself, who puts an end to the reaping concerning the sin we confessed. Therefore, it is necessary that we take action and do our part, thus issuing Him an invitation to do His.

Our confession often involves two things, confessing our sinful response and then forgiving those who may have sinned against us. We are *commanded* to forgive others (Colossians 3:13). To choose not to forgive is sin.

And remember, whenever we confess our sins the Lord also does another very significant thing--He cleanses us from all unrighteousness. In so doing, He removes from our hearts the lingering sinful responses such as bitterness, resentment, judgments, hatred, revenge, etc. Though we may try, in our own power we are unable to remove the unrighteousness in us; but He *is* able, willing and *so very much wanting* to do so.

There's another thing I've found that God does when we pray through our past hurtful memories. He removes from us the terrible sting associated with those memories. Those stinging feelings may have haunted us for many years—feelings like shame, self-hatred, dirtiness, ugliness. But when the Lord moves to cleanse us from *all* unrighteousness, He washes away those defiling, lying, biting feelings as well.

When I was molested as a child by a baby sitter, I was affected in many ways. As I began to recall what had happened to me, old, horrible and unpleasant feelings started to surface. It was these feelings that haunted me, affecting what I thought about myself, sex, men and women. But, after praying through those memories, the haunting feelings disappeared along with the lies I had come to believe. They no longer trouble or disturb me, even when I share the story of what happened to me with others. In fact, that story has now become my testimony to what God can do to bring healing.

So in summary, receiving God's forgiveness and cleansing, by confessing our sinful response to root issues, is what sets us free. With this understanding, we now have something we can *do* with the root issues we come to identify. And, we do this through prayer to the one who witnessed it all and has the power to redeem it. This is what I call the "Pray Through It" model. Keep in mind, this is not a formula but merely some key guidelines to follow when praying through root issues. I have found these to be very helpful, especially since they incorporate both the mind and heart into the process. And further, when we pray out loud, this involves our bodies as well.

The elements of "Pray Through It" are as follows:
- Tell the Lord what happened (Ps. 142:2).
- Share with the Lord how you felt (Ps. 62:8; Heb. 4:15-16).
- Confess to the Lord your sinful responses (Ps. 38:18; I Jn 1:9).
- Forgive those who wronged you (Matt. 6:12-15; Eph. 4:32).
- Renounce any sinful, negative decisions you may have made (2 Cor. 10:5).
- Receive prayer for forgiveness and healing (James 5:16).

Telling the Lord what happened allows us to share what we know from our mind—the recollection of the painful events. This is *our* version of the story. This part confirms our experience by identifying the root issues associated with the bad fruit, and by clarifying what tempted us to make our sinful response.

Sharing with the Lord how you felt allows your heart to feel heard—heard by those with whom you are praying and by the One you are praying to, your Heavenly Father. Most root issues contain a piece which concerns your heart not feeling heard at the time of your wounding. Therefore, this part is especially important

Confessing to the Lord your sinful responses towards others and/or your situation involves your will. This allows you to acknowledge your part in what happened and that you are responsible for your sinful responses regardless of what happened.

Forgiving those who wronged you involves your will as well, and allows you to release those who hurt you. Yet more importantly, it restores your sense of choice--that you are not, nor do you have to remain, a victim.
Renouncing any sinful negative decisions gives you the opportunity to give up the lies you may have come to believe and exchange them for what God says is true.

Receiving prayer for forgiveness and healing involves your willingness to humble yourself to receive God's blessing through another.

The following are some additional thoughts on the basic elements of "Pray Through It." More could be said, but what has been provided is helpful in getting started.

Tell the Lord What Happened

When telling the Lord what happened, we need to share our perspective. Perhaps we had assumed something or didn't know all the facts at the time. Strong emotional moments have a way of magnifying our circumstances, accentuating certain details and tempting use to jump to conclusions. When we do make judgments, we often do so based upon what we *thought* we knew to be true, which may not have been a completely accurate assessment of the situation. Yet, even if our assessment wasn't right on we are still bound to bear bad fruit anyway because of our sinful response to it.

For instance, as a child I came to resent my mother the day she dropped me off at kindergarten. It was time for me to start going to

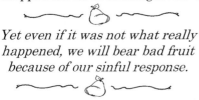

Yet even if it was not what really happened, we will bear bad fruit because of our sinful response.

school and she needed to go to work. Yet, I misperceived her leaving me as rejection. Yes, it is valid that I did not want to go to school that day. And also, perhaps I was predisposed to rejection because of my parent's divorce. But the result was that I chose a sinful response which planted a seed that later bore the repeated bad fruit of rejection in my life.

Sometimes, all we know about a root issue is a few sketchy details or a story someone told us. Perhaps in prayer, the Lord revealed a little more but we still don't feel like we have a whole lot of evidence to go on. If this is the case, try praying through it anyway.

Remember, if you have enough details that the root issue seems plausible then run with it, and let the Lord sort it out. What I do in these instances is offer what I call an "if-prayer". An "if-prayer" goes something like this, "Lord, if _____ did really happen then I would have felt _____ and would have resented _____ for what they did." When we do this, we are praying by faith through a root issue with what facts we have even if we may not be completely sure. If we pray though something in this manner and it effects change in our life, great! And if nothing changes, there is no loss. But if we don't pray through it, we will never know.

A husband and wife came to me to deal with some marital problems they were having. It became apparent that their bad fruit theme was around reaping stress in many areas of their lives. As we explored more it was apparent that the stress was especially prevalent in the husband's work. The stress was considerably more than normal and it never seemed to go away. The husband had resigned himself to live and work around it even though it drove his wife crazy. The husband even shared that as far back as he could remember he had an ulcer that never went away. It would just flare-up once in awhile when the stress got very intense. What was interesting is that he was told that he was even *born* with it!

When asked what he knew about what was going on while he was in the womb, he shared a story he was told by his mother. Though his mother wanted him, the pregnancy, itself, caused her a great deal of stress. She was overweight, and it was very hot where they lived. Though she loved the fact that she was going to have a baby, she was miserable because of her discomfort. All she could think about was getting through the pregnancy so she could find relief.

Since the story fit the bad fruit, I then led him to pray through it with an "if-prayer." It went something like this, "Lord, while in the womb I might have felt my mother's stress. If so, I know I would not have liked it, especially if it went on and on and there was no relief. I also may have felt pressured to be born. As a result, I may have resented my mother for this. If I did, I confess my resentment as sin and I choose to forgive my mother." Since there was no apparent negative decision made, there was nothing to renounce.

After he prayed, I then asked the Lord to heal his ulcer. As a result, we saw some very tangible changes. For one, his ulcer went away, right then and there! When I saw him six months later, it was *still* gone, and he had had it for 45 years! But on top of this, the stress in his business decreased. He even remarked that his foremen no longer seemed jumpy around him (i.e., they too were less stressed).

Another detail you should know, is that until he came in for help, his business kept going further and further into debt each year despite his efforts. Yet, within six months of praying the "if-prayer", his business' debt had dropped by more than 80%! Talk about less stress!

Share with the Lord How You Felt

The Lord wants us to pour out our hearts, to share with Him what we experienced. The Psalms are filled with examples of this. Often, the writer shared exactly how he felt even if it seemed to contradict what he knew to be true. And, isn't this when we most often need to share and be heard, when things don't seem to

So often we move too quickly to "doing the right thing"...

make sense? Isn't this when we need God's mercy and grace the most? If you'll notice in the Psalms, it was *after* sharing his pain that the writer was able to acknowledge the truth and praise the Lord, despite his feelings.

So often we move too quickly to "doing the right thing"—such as confessing, forgiving, and renouncing. Don't get me wrong. These *are* right things to do, but often we do them at the expense of our own hearts by not allowing ourselves to express our feelings. Whenever we do this, we actually invalidate our feelings, treating ourselves with no more sensitivity than those who hurt us in the first place.

Most unresolved issues involve legitimate needs not met (or violated) and feelings invalidated (or never expressed). God truly wants us to share our experiences, so that our hearts will feel honored and validated. And, He wants us to know that we are *worth* the time and effort needed to process these issues and be heard.

I'll let you in on a little secret. Pouring out your heart to the Lord *is* part of doing the "right thing". Tell Him what you

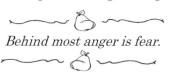

Behind most anger is fear.

experienced and how you felt when you were hurt or disappointed. Share with Him what lies you came to believe, and why. Don't worry. The truth of God's love, His forgiveness, His grace and His mercy won't go away just because you are expressing how you feel. Jesus is the Truth-- He is truth personified. And He does not change.

Besides, we can't hide anything from the Lord. So, we might as well admit how we truly feel. He feels what you feel and He is not threatened by it. He knows how much you need to be heard. He is waiting for you to be honest with yourself and with Him. This is what integrity is—being real and genuine with what we feel before God while not moving to the point of resentment and sin.

We may have actually dishonored our past feelings by not acknowledging them appropriately. Perhaps there was no safe way to do so under the circumstances. We may have been punished when we did express ourselves by being verbally or physically reprimanded, shamed or even ignored. Through all of this, we may have actually "trained" ourselves not to feel. Thus, we no longer know what we really do feel.

If we are sad, that needs to be expressed as sadness. If we need to cry, then it needs to come out as crying. An inability or unwillingness to cry may keep our emotions from being expressed and again be an indication of bad fruit.

Behind most anger is fear— fear that we won't be heard, loved or acknowledged -- that some realistic and felt need may not be met. If it wasn't safe to be afraid or share our fears as a child, we may have decided to deny our fears. Thus, we now get angry as a protection in order to keep others from knowing that we really are afraid.

Pray Through It

Being depressed is not, in itself, wrong nor is it necessarily bad fruit. However, if someone has a pattern of depression in their life or seems to get "stuck" in it, this could be bad fruit. Depression is often a sign of "emotional tiredness". When we are depressed, a lot of emotional reserves and energy are being used up and drained away in order to keep unexpressed emotions hidden.

When it comes to our feelings, most of us have a very limited vocabulary. Perhaps we grew up in homes where feelings were not shared, were ignored or maybe where only certain feelings were

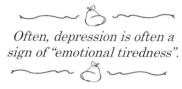

Often, depression is often a sign of "emotional tiredness".

"allowed". As a result, we lack experience in expressing ourselves.

When I was a child, my emotional vocabulary was limited to three words-- I felt "good", "bad" or "sad." Since at the time I was not able to acknowledge or recognize other feelings, my mind learned to compensate for my heart. For instance, joy to me became more of an attitude, a way of perceiving life and not necessarily a feeling. As an adult looking back, I realize now that I was often depressed as a child though I didn't even recognize it at the time. This revelation came as the Lord began to restore my heart. Remember, a mind that works overtime is frequently one whose owner is trying hard to avoid or keep from feeling. It is trying to do what only the heart can do—identify and express feelings.

I have found that, while praying through something, if you speak out how you felt at the time, your heart will feel affirmed and heard. If you don't remember how you felt, go ahead and speak out what you *may* have thought you felt. Ask yourself, "How would someone have felt if what happened to me had happened to them?" Often, it is a good idea to spend time with someone else who can help you clarify these things. The more you do this, the more your heart will be restored. It's like inviting your heart to share again--wooing it out little by little. Greater clarification will come as your heart becomes more restored and as your "feeling" vocabulary enlarges. In the process of praying through your bitter roots, remember, your heart needs to be encouraged to do its job—to tell you how you feel. As you honor your heart by speaking out a feeling, your heart begins to be restored, and the feelings begin to come.

Though helpful, it is not *necessary* to be emotional when you pray through memories. If the feelings are there, then express them. But, don't hold back on praying through it if the feelings don't come. Just the process of sharing how you *may have felt* starts something, which is especially helpful for people who can't seem to feel anything. There have been a number of occasions where I have seen the disappearance of bad fruit after praying through an issue despite a lack of demonstrated emotion. One such example is the man mentioned earlier who had the ulcer!

Confess to the Lord Your Sinful Responses

Confession is acknowledging our choices. It is admitting our sinful responses regardless of what may have happened to us or what others may have done. In some cases, we may have felt we had no other choice. But, that's what's so wonderful about God's grace and mercy. It is there for us to receive without condemnation regardless of why or how we responded. God is excited to have us confess because it means He can forgive us and our relationship with Him will be restored.

Sometimes while praying through root issues, we may need to confess other sins that we have committed from the motivation of

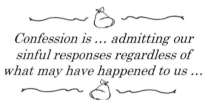

Confession is … admitting our sinful responses regardless of what may have happened to us …

that root issue. What I am referring to here are things like addictions, lies, adultery, outbursts of rage. Despite the fact that we know where they came from, they are sins in and of themselves, and need to be confessed as such. Even though we thought we had a good reason for turning to those behaviors, we were not forced to do them. We were tempted and chose against self-control. We sinned. And we need to take responsibility for that.

Forgive Those Who Wronged You

Forgiveness is a choice, not a feeling. If it were a feeling, many of us would probably never get around to it. It is actually acknowledgement that though what the other person did may have been wrong, we choose to no longer hold them accountable to us for it. It is our way of releasing them to the Lord,

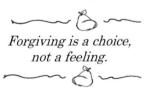

Forgiving is a choice, not a feeling.

and moving to trust Him with them and with what they have done.

At times, we all find it very difficult to forgive. We want to, but for some reason it seems too hard or even impossible. In such instances, we need to ask the Lord to help us. And He will help us!

Take for instance the man in Mark 9: 21-27 who asked Jesus to take pity and heal his son. When Jesus said to the man, "Everything is possible to him who believes", the man immediately said, "I do believe; help me overcome my unbelief." In response Jesus didn't say, "I'm sorry but that's not good enough. Well, I'll tell you what. Once you believe 100% then I will see what I can do for you." No, instead he honored the man's honesty and the measure of belief he did have, and Jesus healed his son.

Remember, to not forgive is sin. But, as mentioned before, don't just jump right to forgiving, share with Lord what happened and how it made you feel. And then forgive.

Renounce Any Sinful Negative Decisions

Often, when we are hurt it is because a lie comes to battle against us such as, "You're no good" or, "You can't do anything right." And then, after being hurt and resenting those who treated us badly, those lies become personalized, taking the form of, "I'm no good" or, "I can't do anything right." In some cases, we might add our own lies to the list such as, "No body loves me" and, "There is no use in trying." What's worse is when these lies don't seem to go away. They become ingrained in us, they persist, they defy the truth we once knew and set up a new reality in our hearts.

These negative decisions are what are known as strongholds, and in this case, personal negative strongholds. They are personal in that they are ours. They are formed out of our personal experience and remain because they are associated

...negative strongholds ... keep us bound-up under the oppression of the lies upon which they are based.

with our root issues. They are negative in that they keep us bound-up under the oppression of the lies upon which they are based.

What God wants us to do is to tear down these arguments or imaginations and those things that have been raised up against the knowledge of Him (II Corinthians 10:5). And what is the knowledge of God? For starters, it is everything that is based upon His truth and His character. This would be such truths as "God loves me" when the lie I accepted is that "no one loves me." Therefore, personal destructive strongholds are those things that are not based upon God's truth and His character. When dealing with bad fruit, these will be in keeping with it.

Which brings us to the last part of praying through root issues — "tearing down" or demolishing our negative decisions. These are our personal negative strongholds. We tear them down by taking back our negative decisions, giving them up, or renouncing them. When doing so, we use whatever words we find appropriate that express our choice to give up that decision: "I renounce...", "I give up...", "I no longer agree with the lie that..." or "I take back..."

For instance, if we renounce the lie that "no body loves me", we do so in recognition that *God* loves us, since it is not true that "*no body* loves me." In so doing, we are choosing to believe God's truth about us in exchange for the lies our heart chose to believe.

Receiving Prayer for Forgiveness and Healing

God uses us to bless one another. Though it is God who forgives us and heals us, He uses our prayers for one another to bring this about. (James 5:16)

When we confess our sins out loud, we have the privilege of re-assuring each other of God's forgiveness. If, in the reading of this book, you have prayed through a root issue, you should now share about it with someone you trust so they can pray God's forgiveness over you. There is something wonderful about someone pronouncing God's forgiveness over us. I know for myself, that I am so much more apt to *feel* forgiven when someone prays for me and makes such a pronouncement. Somehow it seems more real.

Your friend may want to add to their prayer to cover any specific fears or doubts you may have concerning your walk from this point forward. We all benefit from prayers requesting and re-assuring us of God's love, presence and provision. Perhaps they can pray verses over us that are in keeping with these things and the truth we have accepted in exchange for the lies we once believed.

There is something wonderful about someone pronouncing God's forgiveness over us.

In prayer, I will often ask the Lord to bring along circumstances and people that will draw out and reinforce the truth in the healing that has just taken place. It's also a good idea to ask the Lord to remind the individual of the new truths written in their heart when the old lies come knocking. Because, often they will.

I have a friend who draws pictures while a person is identifying and praying through root issues. She does this during the counseling session as the Lord shows her specific things about each person. Often these pictures are of the person with Jesus while He does something amazing and special with them. It is remarkable how encouraging these pictures are, especially weeks later when the person goes home and is tempted by the enemy to take back the old garbage. Looking at them again reminds them of the truth of what happened in the prayer session, and that that truth remains as solidly as the Lord who brought it.

Further, if there was demonic harassment associated with a root issue, I suggest that you have someone ask the Lord in prayer to remove it. Likewise, if after dealing with a root the individual is drained and exhausted, the friend can pray for rest and restoration.

We often need prayer for healing from anything that was associated with the bad fruit, things that had resulted from the now prayed through root issues. They should also pray for whatever blessings would build you up in contrast to the ways the bad fruit tore you down. If it involved relationships, you might need prayers for restoration of trust. If it was related to your work, self-perspective, finances, sleep, or something else, it is a good idea to have someone pray for you concerning those specific things. Perhaps your bad fruit was connected to a physical ailment--ask God to heal it. Lastly, ask your friend to spend some time just listening to the Lord, as He might put on their heart something specific, over and above those things, to pray for you.

One last thing I like to do with my clients is give them an assignment. Ideally, this would be something that would foster the truth they exchanged for any lies they may have renounced. God wants us to be transformed by *renewing our minds* (Romans 12:1). And in so doing, we need to discipline ourselves to think upon those things that are good, right, pure, etc. (Philippians 4:8). Whether you create such an assignment for someone else, or they create it for you, it should invite the individual to recall the truth, as stated in God's word, when faced with the old lies.

Pray Through It

Now is the time! Go find that person you trust. Share with them what you have discovered about your bad fruit and bitter root issues to this point. Then in prayer, go through the steps outlined above—and see what happens!

Things to Cultivate

- How many words are in your emotional vocabulary? If there's only a few, what are they, and why do you think they are so few?

- What stories from your past do you know that have similarities to some bad fruit to your life? Ask the Lord for clarification as to what happened, how you felt, what your sinful response was, who was involved, and what the decisions were that you made as a result.

- Are there some things that you have found hard to forgive? With another person, discuss why it is so hard to forgive. And then, when you are ready, choose to forgive anyway, all the while asking the Lord for His grace to do so.

Identifying Your Feelings

The following exercise will help you better identify your feelings. As you practice this over time, your ability to identify and describe your feelings will increase. If possible, do this exercise with a friend. Remember, learning to identify feelings is like learning new words. The more we use them, the more familiar they become, and the quicker we learn to recognize them. For, just as with a larger vocabulary we are able to share ideas with greater clarity, so with a greater palette of emotions our experience of life becomes more colorful and vivid.

Starting with an identified root issue, do the following:
1. Complete the *first* blank of: "It really hurt when _____ happened. I felt _____."
2. While pondering "...I felt _____", slowly scan the list in Appendix A – "Feeling Words"
3. Complete the *second* blank by writing down as many of the words that best describe how you may have felt.
4. Do this for each identified root issue.

Exhibit Good Fruit

He will be like a tree firmly planted by streams of water,
Which yields its fruit in season,
And its leaf does not wither.
And in whatever he does, he prospers.
Psalms 1:3 (NASB)

Produce fruit in keeping with repentance.
Matt. 3:8

God wants us to bear good fruit.

When our lives do bring forth good fruit, it reveals God's glory through and in us. We also experience some good benefits from it. You see, God wants things to go well for us. He wants good fruit to manifest in our relationships so that we begin to see and experience Him and others as they *really* are, and not as our

> *When our lives to bring forth good fruit, it reveals God's glory through and in us.*

prior woundings make them out to be. He desires that we move beyond the muck of our pasts and bear good fruit despite what our circumstances may be.

Exhibiting positive change and good fruit in our lives, after praying through root issues, happens in one of two ways. One way is a natural by-product of the process of praying through root issues. The second way requires our effort.

Change as a Natural Outcome
The natural outcome of praying through root issues is good fruit. Change comes. This is not something we have to necessarily make happen. Nor do we have to believe harder or hope with more effort in order for it to appear. The good fruit will happen on its own.

After praying through something, the root feeding the bad fruit has been cut off--yanked out. This results in the reduction of bad fruit bearing. As for the growth of good fruit, it comes from sowing good seeds, like obedience. So, when we obey God by confessing our sins, by forgiving others, and by giving up lies in exchange for truth, we are sowing good seeds, seeds of obedience. The result is good fruit.

Sometimes we may find that, even after praying through some apparent root issues, nothing seems to change. There can be several reasons for this. When working through the themes of bad fruit in our lives, there is often more than one issue associated with each theme. In some instances, before change comes, several or even many root issues along the same theme will need to be prayed through.

It's like removing a wall. We can smash out bricks here and there but the wall remains. There are gaping holes, to be sure.

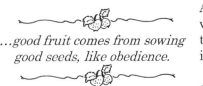

...good fruit comes from sowing good seeds, like obedience.

And, the wall is definitely weakened. But, sometimes it takes a whole lot of demolition for it to finally come crashing down. Sometimes the change comes gradually, growing in strength over time. With each additional issue being prayed through, so each additional change comes. This is often seen in areas where we had a very predominate theme of bad fruit with multiple insults over a long period of time.

Other times, the change will not be seen or felt until later. It often takes a specific circumstance to reveal the change that has taken place. Otherwise, we would never notice it. For instance, it took me getting into an actual argument with my wife for me to realize that I wasn't passive anymore.

However, there are times that the issue we addressed in prayer was in fact not a root issue at all. Just because something adverse happened to us doesn't mean it is a root issue which is producing bad fruit. Again, what causes the bad fruit is the way we responded to what happened. Nevertheless, it is always better to pray through something rather than not, just because we are not sure.

Many times, just after praying, some people feel an immediate release in their hearts. Some experience a change in how they look at life, themselves, others, and even God. A typical response is that the pain in one's heart is gone, like something has been lifted off.

On more than one occasion, I have seen clients who were very skilled at trying to use logic to reason their way through their issues, unsuccessfully of course. They had trained their minds to believe the best about a situation though their hearts never really bought it. But, when they finally prayed through the issue, their hearts were released to *feel* the truth they once only *knew*.

I remember one woman sharing about what had happened in relation to her father after praying through some of her issues. She said, "The things my father continues to do no longer 'get to me', even though I may still hurt." It may still hurt when people hurt us, but when the heart issues have been addressed, it no longer *goes deep* as it once did. It 's also easier to let those offenses go.

Often, after praying through root issues, we may experience a true sense of peace for the first time in our lives. Shame, guilt and despair melt away. Lies are lifted. Recurring bad dreams cease. It becomes easier to receive God's grace and His presence, and to hear His voice. Things look brighter, life feels a little easier to walk through—we feel less burdened. Like a weight has been lifted off us. We see things differently. Each change brings benefits that are unique to the individual and their root issues.

Sometimes though, we may experience tiredness and even exhaustion after praying through our issues. This is very normal.

Her changed heart now made their bad fruit more evident...

In fact, it's often evidence that something deep in our hearts has been accomplished. When this happens, it's a good idea to get some rest—take a nap, or two!

There may be an adjustment period, a falling-out, or a felt change in our relationships. This can be a bit of a shock for some of us. For others, this might be a relief. This is because the theme of the root issue has been addressed in prayer. As a result, certain people no longer "match", or fit, our root issues anymore--and we no longer fit theirs. In addition, we may no longer want to be around certain people anymore. Or, we may simply discover that we attract a different type of individual—one who wants a healthy, not a dysfunctional, relationship.

One lady I knew had a history of struggling with an inability to assert herself. Prior to getting help, she had been easily manipulated, and people took advantage of her. This was the bad fruit that caused her to want counseling. Yet, after praying through her root issues around this, God restored her ability to say "no" and to say it without feeling guilty or bad. To her surprise, within the first few weeks of returning home her business partners came to her asking that she leave their partnership. The reason why: they could no longer manipulate her and get her to do all the work. Her changed heart made *their* bad fruit more evident. Now, this was actually a God-given opportunity for them—to rise to the occasion and change. However, they didn't see it as such, and chose to flee the relationship to seek another person whom they could easily manipulate. Either way, it was a blessing to my client, as she moved on to healthier and more profitable work relationships.

If we are single, we may find ourselves becoming attracted to a different spectrum of individuals from the opposite sex. Our preferences may change. Why? Because our root issues are gone, and we are now less likely to be attracted to those who were in keeping with our root issues.

Sometimes friendships and even engagements have been broken off because one person began to deal with roots, while the other did not. One young man, after praying through the main issues in his life, saw a change in his relationships when he went back to college. He and one of his previous friends began to drift apart. It was as if they didn't have as much in common any more. Though they were still friends, things didn't seem the same. At first, this was very disconcerting for him. But he soon recognized that this was because he no longer had similar root issues to his friend. What did happen was that he began forming a new close friendship with another guy. This was someone who was more "whole", and who didn't buy in to any of the old lies he once believed about himself.

If we're married, our spouse may seem to change. Because of what has happened in us, our relationship with them may get thrown out of balance. Often, our new feeling of freedom gives our spouses room to change and blossom where they once felt stifled by our defilement. They no longer feel tempted to respond in line with the judgments once rooted in our hearts. Our change may affect them in such a way that they even get in touch with their own unresolved issues. (The first story in the chapter called *Examples of "Praying Through It"* is an example of this.) In some cases, they may become less inclined to blame us, since our defilement is gone, and they find it more difficult to project their issues on us. Or, we may just realize that our spouse's actions and words don't hurt us like they once did.

Often our circumstances will change—we may lose a job or have to move. We may finally get a job we had been trying for so long to land. One man came seeking help while he was in between jobs. His former pattern was that he kept getting jobs where there would be a lot of miscommunication between his bosses and himself. He found that he was "getting in trouble" a lot—doing what he *thought* he was being told to do and then finding out later that his boss actually expected something different of him. Needless to say, this made him feel very nervous, not knowing what he might do that would get him "in trouble." Yet when he prayed through the root issues from his childhood, he reported that his very next job was different. It was a place where he was well informed and knew exactly what to do and not to do. They even paid him for his training time.

Another man kept experiencing being overlooked at his place of employment. Others got raises or opportunities to advance while he didn't, even when he asked. And worse yet, the boss always seemed to have a "reasonable" explanation. Yet, after praying through some of his root issues, he was given the chance to advance and was finally given a raise.

Sometimes, things just have to be "worked through" before there can be change and resolution. As a result of one's prior actions and choices, certain commitments and involvements have already been set in motion. These things will need to be carried out and walked through, regardless of having prayed through root issues. The good part is that, now that they have been addressed, we will most likely not be affected as deeply. In some cases God wants us to remain where we are, to work character in our lives, especially now that a root issue has been addressed.

> *Sometimes, things just have to be "worked through" before there can be change and resolution.*

For a few of us, things seem to actually get more difficult instead of better. This often happens with people who have held their feelings in for many, many years. As their hearts are restored they begin to feel again—and feeling can be very uncomfortable. Because they have held things in so long, they have some catching up to do. And this will often just take some time.

Change That Comes Through Effort

There is a second aspect to exhibiting change, and this is the one that demands effort on our part. This is something that is required of us. It's where *we* bring forth fruit in keeping with what we have repented of (Matthew 3:8). Repentance means to turn the other way, as in "about face, forward march." It is not enough to just turn. We now need to walk in the truth, to actively live it out daily.

> *It is not enough to just turn... We now need to walk in the truth, to actively live it out daily.*

Previously, our heart had been geared towards resenting someone, as we held unforgiveness against that person. That resentment kept us from seeing and admitting our part, which kept us from resolving the issue. We believed lies about ourselves, about others, and about life. But once we turn from these things by praying through them, we need to continue on in the new way.

Once the lies have been removed, we need to walk in the truth and embrace it by reminding our heart of what we now know. Regardless of bad fruit and root issues and how far we have come in the healing process, we need to put into practice the things God would have us do-- resist sin, be self-controlled, pray, and study the Bible to name a few. We need to draw near to Jesus. We also need to draw near to others who will remind us of the truth and encourage us—people we can pray with and confess our secret struggles to.

The Lord told us we would be faced with difficulties and trials in this life (John 16:33). As Christians, we will at times wrestle against old bad habits in the midst of our pursuit of good character and further healing. While in this life, we will continue to battle against Satan and his forces, who would like nothing more than to see us lay down the truth we have come to know for a new set of lies.

Sometimes, there may need to be a period of perseverance or resistance to temptation before there is an experience of lasting change. I remember occasions where, despite having prayed

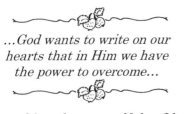

...God wants to write on our hearts that in Him we have the power to overcome...

through some issues, for a time I still had to endure difficulties similar to the pattern of my old bad fruit. But as I hung in there, it eventually lifted off. The Lord was not only building character in my life, He eventually showed me something about myself that I hadn't known. He showed me that I had certain abilities within me that I would have never known of nor developed had I not gone through what I had. Often, the Lord allows such experiences that we might learn a lesson in conquering—that we might learn that His grace is always sufficient—that His power, indeed, is made perfect in our weakness.

Where we once felt defeated, and even controlled, by an issue, God wants to write on our hearts that *in Him* we have the power to overcome it. And further, that when we conquer something, we gain a measure of authority in that area. This newfound authority allows us to do things we never thought we could have. It also allows us the ability to speak into others' lives, helping and encouraging them so they too may become free and more effective in serving the Lord.

Things to Cultivate

Record the Truth

After praying through a root issue, spend some time writing down your answers to the following questions:

- What is the *truth* God says about me? (i.e., "I am worth listening to", "God loves me.")
- What scriptures support this?
- What is a practical way I can actively put into practice the truth of what God says about me?

Record What God Says

As a result of the good fruit that has come, spend time asking the Lord the following questions and write down what He tells you. You will know you have heard Him if what you hear is in keeping with His Word:

- "What do You like about me?"
- "How do You see me?" – He might give you a picture of something, or perhaps He will speak to you more through words than pictures. Take the truth (which you exchanged for the lie you used to believe), and ask the Lord, "Why is this true about me?"

Review Special Insights

Along with what you may have recorded from doing the above, be sure to write down any meaningful word, vision, scripture, song, etc., that the Lord has given you anywhere along the way in the process of your investigation and prayer. From time to time, read these out loud to yourself. Meditate on them, and then write down any further insights you receive. Be sure to encourage yourself with these often.

Write Out Your Story

Record the process that you went through when you prayed through one or more root issues. When you do, be sure to elaborate while answering the following questions:

- What was the bad fruit?
- What were the root issues?
- What was my prayer?
- What was the good fruit that came?

Share Your Story With Others

There are a number of reasons to write out your story. For one, this will be an encouragement to you now, as well as later. It will help you realize what God can do in other areas in your life. But even more so, this will be a testimony you can now share. As you share it, the Lord will use it to encourage and bless others. This has become your "good news" to share with others, and good news is what He uses to reach the world, one person at a time.

Lastly, I would love to hear how the Lord has blessed you. If you feel so inclined, mail or e-mail me with your story. Such stories are always encouraging for me. Be sure to let me know if it is something you might allow me to share with others when ministering, teaching and writing. I look forward to hearing from you!

 RIPE in Review

The following is a summary of **RIPE**. This is helpful to refer to when dealing with bad fruit in your life.

Recognize - recognize the bad fruit
- Make note of the specific kinds bad fruit that you are experiencing.
- Look for a pattern in the times and circumstances when this type of issue has occurred in your life.
- Recall how it made you feel whenever this happened.

Identify - identify the root issues
- Remember, the fruit looks like the root, and if there's bad fruit there's a bad root.
- Ask the Lord to show you other times in your life when you felt this same way.
  - Write these down and include any important details.
  - For each event, list what decisions you made and the lies you came to believe as a result.

Pray Through It – pray through the root issues
For each event, in prayer to the Lord:
- Tell the events of what had happened.
- Share with Him how you felt at the time.
- Confess your sinful responses to the situation.
- Forgive those who wronged you.
- Renounce any sinful, negative decisions you may have made.
- Receive prayer for forgiveness and healing.

Exhibit Good Fruit
- Watch for, and experience, good fruit.
- Put out effort in producing good fruit.

Examples of "Praying Through It"

We're not keeping this to ourselves,
we're passing it along
to the next generation-
GOD's fame and fortune,
the marvelous things he has done.
Psalm 78:4 (MSG)

When God has done great things in our lives, He wants us to share them with others.

If you are like me, I learn so much more from hearing about the real-life experiences of others. Hearing such stories often leads us to reflect on our own lives. And we're encouraged, too, because we gain confidence that something can really be done about our problems. Please be aware that, in most of the stories I am about to share, healing was not necessarily instantaneous, nor did *all* the problems these people had disappear.

Remember, becoming a Christian doesn't mean all the "bad stuff" magically goes away. It does, however, mean that we have a resource in our amazingly gracious and merciful Lord for dealing with that "stuff". And, it especially means that we have Jesus, Himself, to walk through life with us.

As you read through these stories, you will see the key elements I have identified in the book demonstrated as the individuals pray through their roots. You will also notice that there is not a strict "formula" or specific way to pray. Instead, each prayer befits the uniqueness of the individual and the Lord's leading. Though the names of the people involved, as well as other personal information, may have been changed, the actual events, issues and results are true. In addition, the prayers are not necessarily word-for-word but rather a summary of what was prayed.

If you find yourself identifying with some of the following stories, get out your pen and paper and write down what the Lord is showing you. Then, begin to work through RIPE. It is my prayer that the Lord would use these stories to cause you to reflect on your own life. And in so doing, a door of opportunity would be opened to you where the Master Counselor can freely enter and do his beautiful work to make you whole.

No One Asks Me Personal Questions

There was a time when John felt like no one really wanted to get to know him. Others would tell him all about themselves, but no one seemed to take a personal interest in him. John felt like he was the one always asking the questions. Through our time together, we learned that, as a child, he had evidently come to accept this as a norm for himself. But as an adult, he began to realize he held a deep inner resentment inside about it. He often tried to console himself with thoughts like, "I'm just a 'nice guy," or "It's the Christian thing to do." Now, of course, these things are true, but it's also normal and healthy to expect an exchange of interest and thoughts in a relationship. Relationships involve give and take—and he found that his involved a lot of give and not so much take.

As we began to explore where this pattern might have originated, John remembered sitting around the dinner table with his brothers while visiting with their dad. As he remembered it, it seemed like his father did all the talking. As a child, John assumed that this was just what fathers and sons did—dads talk, and sons listen and ask questions. He also remembered that, if he wanted to say anything he couldn't simply wait to be asked, he'd just have to jump in. The problem was, if he did, his father would quickly turn the conversation back to himself. In addition, John told me he couldn't remember his father *ever* asking him a personal question.

So, recognizing this as a possible bitter root John prayed, "Lord, I remember how my brothers and I would sit around the table while my dad did all the talking. When we did speak up, he would quickly bring the conversation back to himself. I needed him to ask me personal questions and take an interest in me. And, I see now that I judged him for it. I resented him for not making me feel important. I began to believe that my job was just to listen and ask questions. As a result, I felt rejected. What I see now is that I gave up, and accepted lies in order to deal with my disappointment. I now forgive him for keeping my brothers and me in those roles and for not showing interest in us. I also give up my decision that I cannot expect anyone to ask me personal questions."

Result

Part I: Soon after our session together, John's father phoned him. Out of habit, he prepared himself to do a lot of listening--but then something different happened. He actually asked John two questions: "How are you doing?" and "How is work going?" He couldn't believe it! Remembering what he had prayed, he took that window of opportunity and began sharing. Something had changed. As a matter of fact, John has since shared with me that whenever he has a conversation with his father now, his dad almost always asks one or two personal questions. You see, John's father didn't change—he did. His judgment is gone, no longer tempting his father to ignore him.

Part II: When John shared with his wife what had changed between his father and him, it really touched *her* heart—so much so, that she went into their bedroom and began crying. Later, when John asked her what happened, she shared that she had remembered how much it hurt when *her* father did not take an interest in her as a child. Evidently, sharing his story got her in touch with her buried pain. So, while in the bedroom remembering her hurt, he led her to pray through her memories and the judgments she had made towards her dad.

About two days later, her father called. Though he had called in the passed, this time it was different. In the past John observed their conversations as being always brief. But this time she actually had a conversation with him that lasted over a half-an-hour! So you see, the good fruit in John's life became a catalyst, encouraging healing in his wife's life as well.

It Won't Last

When Susan moved into her newly-built home, she felt overwhelmed. Something about it was too much for her, and she couldn't rest in it. She found it hard to "receive" her new home, and what should have been joyful left her feeling uneasy. Moreover, there was another pressing though very different issue in Susan's life. Although she was generally able to have an "open" heart when communicating with her husband, he noticed that if while they were talking something came to upset her, she would immediately close down and throw up a wall between them. He shared how much this hurt and asked if she realized she was doing this. Although hard to admit, she agreed and decided to take this issue to prayer. Her husband prayed, "Jesus, will you show us when Susan learned to close her heart?" And the Lord brought the following to her mind.

Susan was born in Germany during World War II. As a little girl she and her family had survived the bombing of Dresden in February, 1945. Because of the devastation, her family went to stay on a dairy farm in Bavaria. This place became a haven for her. She bonded deeply to the farmer's wife who became like a grandmother to her. This was a real gift to Susan since her own mother, though physically present, had been so traumatized by the war that she was unable to give her much attention.

Pray Through It

But then the Lord went on to show her something else. All this came to an end when Susan was 4 ½ years old. She saw herself waving good-bye to "Grandma" as her parents just up and left the farm and moved to Argentina. Her heart was torn in two. She was leaving a safe haven (and a mother-figure she had bonded with) and going to an unknown place with her real mother, who was empty and hurting inside, and her father who was not sensitive to her emotional needs. As a result, she had decided to shut down emotionally, convinced that close, loving relationships "will never last" and that she'd "always lose."

Susan's husband then asked, "Would it be okay to ask Jesus to take to the cross your need to close your heart when you feel scared that you might lose or that nothing good will last?"

In response she began to cry, saying, "What will I do when I get hurt again?" Her choice to close off was further reinforced by wounding from her father while in Argentina. He had made it very difficult for her to keep her heart open to him. Though she had previously prayed through these issues regarding her father, she had not touched the pain from when her family had left the farm.

So in prayer, Susan shared with the Lord how much she hated what had happened back then and how much it had hurt her. She confessed her decision to close her heart and willing released that to Him. This allowed the grief which had been buried for all those years to surface.

As a result, Susan found that the impulse to close down emotionally whenever she felt hurt was subsiding. It now had become more of a choice than an automatic response. She found the strength to hand in and communicate rather than run away, which made a great difference in her marriage. In addition, she could finally rest in her new home, for it no longer reminded her heart of the time when she was taken away from the farm and the "grandmother" she loved.

I Have Too Much to Say

While Kelly and I were working together to prepare a talk that she was going to give at a conference, she found it very difficult to organize her thoughts. She began to feel a lot of emotions coming up, especially as she tried to rehearse what she would say.

When I asked what she thought was behind the feelings, she said she felt like she had too much to share. Being a fellow counselor well-versed in looking for roots she immediately took that thought to the Lord and asked Him to show her when else she had felt like this and who made her feel this way. She remembered being in school as a child and having a teacher who was very harsh and critical at her every attempt to write a composition or do an oral report. She had observed him treating other students this same way, which caused many of the kids to be afraid they would be corrected, even though they did just as he asked them to. As she pondered this memory, Kelly realized that not only had she been offended, herself, but she had also taken offense for another student for the way he was treated. In addition to judging the teacher, she had judged herself for having "too much to say," thus agreeing with the criticism the teacher had given her. She also discovered that she had made several other negative decisions such as "I have nothing good to say", "I ask stupid questions", "I don't know how to express myself" and the like. When we asked the Lord what He thought about this, He told Kelly that she had a *storehouse* of good things to share, which came from what He had taught her as well as from her personal experiences. In addition, He *wanted* her to share these things with others, and He would show her which things to share.

In prayer, Kelly related her story about what happened at school, how much it had hurt her, and how it had caused her to feel bad about what she shared. She confessed her sin of judging the teacher and forgave him for how he had hurt her and the other students, especially the one boy. She then listed all the negative decisions she had made, confessing them as sin and choosing to renounce them.

After this, Kelly and I returned to preparing for the conference. She felt the difference immediately. She found that not only could she come up with pertinent insights, she could express them easily as well. And, she was able to do this without a lot of deep emotions distracting her. When she finally did give her talk, she did *very* well, without any fears creeping up that she had "too much to say."

She's Mad, I Must Be Bad

While visiting together, Michael and his friend discussed all sorts of interesting things. They talked about personal convictions, movies, current events, politics, and other issues. It was a good time, but as Michael was leaving, he felt an old familiar heaviness come upon him. He described the feeling as one which told him that he was "bad" somehow. And, that this was related to when he and his friend were sharing their personal convictions. Though Michael is a strong Christian, he feels freedom in some areas his friend does not, and this resulted in Michael feeling haunted by an unspoken sense of condemnation after their time together.

Later on that day, Michael said he talked with his wife on the phone. The "bad" feeling was still hanging over him. Through their conversation, he could tell that something was wrong and that she was mad at him. Suddenly, the feeling changed from, "I'm bad" to "It must be my fault that she's mad." The problem was, Michael didn't know what he did wrong and so didn't know how to fix it! Unfortunately, this was a common pattern in their communication style and what finally led Michael to come in for help.

In prayer, Michael asked the Lord to reveal other times he had felt this way. The Lord showed him several instances, particularly in his relationship with his father. Michael recalled how his father never seemed to get excited about him or take interest in him. As his parents were divorced, he didn't see his father very often, and when he did, his dad always seemed to have something else on his mind. As Michael reflected on how this made him feel, a deep sense of sadness welled up within him, and he began to cry. As a son, he needed his dad to *want* to know him, to care about his likes and dislikes, his latest accomplishments, his discoveries. But, that lack of interest instead just left a gaping hole in Michael's heart—a hole that made him vulnerable to others' opinions of him, no matter how warped they may be.

Michael then prayed through all these memories and feelings of how his father didn't make him feel special or loved. He then confessed the judgments he held against him, and forgave him. Lastly, he renounced his decision that he was "not special", and that no one would see him as such.

At that point, Michael made the connection between what had happened with his dad when he was younger and the present day theme he was struggling with—"She's mad, I must be bad." If his father *had* thought he was wonderful, and he really knew this in his heart, then when others would imply that he was "bad" in some way, he would be less likely to let their opinion affect him. But because, in truth, his heart was left empty in this area, he was vulnerable to believing the lie that he must *be* bad, not that he sometimes did bad things. Whenever he would see his mother get angry, especially since his parents were divorced, he somehow came to think it was his fault and that he had to fix it. Because he couldn't, he concluded as a child that he was "bad". This shows how important it is that children really know they are a delight to their parents, especially their fathers.

As result of praying through this, Michael reported that the old heavy feeling lifted. He also found a new sense of freedom, freedom from an inappropriate sense of responsibility when his wife got upset. Over time, this led to better communication between them, since Michael was less defensive and more open to her. And this, in turn, has caused her to feel more listened to and therefore valued.

No Longer Responsible

Lynette had been struggling with a pattern of unhealthy relationships, most of the time with women. These women gave her a sense of safety in the relationship and made her feel good about herself, something she could not find elsewhere. She often sought out "exclusive relationships" where they would not have any friends except for each other. But this type of relationships eventually led to problems.

While Lynette was growing up, she remembered her mother as being very controlling and manipulative. She often referred to Lynette as "the child of my old age," which meant "this is the child who will take care of me when I am old". In essence she would buy Lynette's attention by frequently giving her gifts—gifts with a long string attached. Lynette told me, "I grew up feeling bought, like a prostitute. I was 'mommy's little girl' and I knew I'd have to lose part of myself to make it through life." Everything was about Mom—a mom who imposed on Lynette the lie that she was born to take care of her mother.

So we asked the Lord about this and He revealed that, while Lynette was in the womb, her mother had times of being very distraught. She would sometimes scream at the top of her lungs and then fall down crying, because of some unresolved traumatic issues. Because this was ongoing and so troubling Lynette had decided she would just have to take care of her mother, be strong, and not complain.

As a result, we could see how Lynette's identity and purpose became entangled in her mother's well-being. She did not know who she was apart from her mother, and she found it difficult to form relationships other than with "needy" people. What compounded the problem was that her mother gave her lots of affirmation for this quality of tending to needs, which made it difficult for Lynette to step away and become her own person.

The wonderful thing was how the Lord, in a vision, showed Lynette how much He loved her by putting His hands around her while she was in the womb. This signified that she *was* her own person whom He honored and adored. In addition, the Lord revealed the truth that her purpose in life was to love Jesus and delight in Him.

So Lynette prayed through how she had felt, taking on the massive responsibility of caring for her mom. She prayed through all the ways this sense of over-responsibility had been reinforced throughout the years. She renounced her false purpose in life (to take care of Mom) as well as all the other decisions she had made. She then forgave her mother and confessed her judgments against her. Because she had taken on a "purpose" she was not created for, she failed. So she also confessed that she had condemned herself for that failure. She finally was able to see that it wasn't her job in the first place! She also forgave her father for not doing his job (taking care of his wife) and for not protecting her from Mom.

After that, a revelation came into Lynette's heart. She sat there in wonder and asked, "You mean I really don't have to be responsible just because someone has a need?!" Because she was obligated to be responsible for her mother, she felt the same towards others who were needy. Now, after praying through these issues, she felt *free*, not obligated, to care for others.

Wild Horses

When Julie and Ellen started a counseling ministry together, one of the first things they did was travel around the country ministering to others. They were able to effectively help people pray through past issues in their lives. After six weeks of seeing the Lord bring healing to many hearts, Julie became really excited. This whole adventure seemed to be a very real confirmation that she and Ellen were doing the right thing. But Ellen didn't share her excitement. When Ellen shared with Julie, "I'm not sure if I'm called to this ministry," it triggered something in Julie. She had committed herself to this, and now Ellen wasn't sure! Julie felt devastated and became very upset. She put it this way, "It was like someone had cut my mainsail with a sword!" Instead of trying to work through this together, Julie began to slowly withdraw from Ellen.

When they finally got home from their travels, Julie began to receive invitations to travel and minister, but Ellen did not. This made Ellen feel left out and somehow "less-than". It was especially difficult because, by this time, she had worked through her doubt and now felt convinced that she *was* to be a part of this ministry with Julie. This whole situation confused Julie, too, for if the two were to minister together, why wasn't Ellen being invited?

Then something else happened that made things even more confusing for Julie. Someone told a friend of Julie's that she didn't think Julie was committed to what she was doing. This didn't make any sense. She had demonstrated that she was, but now she was being told she was not.

Sometime later, while ministering together in another state, the people Julie and Ellen were staying with took them out to see some wild horses, something Julie had always wanted to do. This was very special for her. And, in fact, three horses even approached Julie. Now this could actually have been very dangerous because they were wild horses. But at that moment the Lord spoke to Julie saying, "This is okay. I have ordained this for you." And to her amazement, the horses came within twelve feet of her and then walked on past. What an unexpected and wonderful experience!

The Lord used this to get Julie in touch with a past issue she had with her father. When she was a little girl, she always wanted a horse. She loved horses so much that she would often dress up in her cowboy outfit with a hat and a rope. Every year, when her birthday came around, she would ask for a horse. And every year she was told, "We can't get one."

One day Julie's father asked her, "Would you like to go on a ride with me? Would you like to go look at a horse?" Julie couldn't believe it. Could this be the day? Was her father really going to buy her a horse? They went to a place where there was a horse named "Red". Julie loved him, and she got to ride him, too. But when she got back into the truck with her dad, she already knew the answer to the question in her heart. Her father started in, "Now, how would you ever take care of him? Eventually, you will just get tired of him." He said some other discouraging things as well. Julie was heartbroken. Basically, the message she got from her father was "you're not trustworthy." In other words, "I don't believe you can follow through on a commitment." And so she judged herself as not able to be responsible for what she loved.

Realizing this, Julie then took to the Lord this whole incident concerning her father. She shared her hurt about not being trusted to take care of what she really wanted. She confessed her judgments against him and forgave him. She also asked God to forgive her for withdrawing. In addition, she gave up the judgment against herself that "I can't be trusted to be responsible for something I love."

Ellen, too, discovered some root issues that were playing into this dynamic between herself and Julie. When Ellen was a little girl, her sisters would always leave her out. She wasn't allowed to join in their games or the fun times they were having with their friends. This made her feel excluded and "less-than," just as she had felt when others were inviting Julie but not her to come and minister. In response to this realization Ellen prayed and shared with Jesus how much it hurt when her sisters excluded her. She then confessed her judgments and forgave her sisters.

As a result, the discouraging force between Julie and Ellen disappeared. Not only did Ellen no longer feel left out, she began to be invited along on ministry trips. As for Julie, she no longer doubts her level of commitment to something she loves. Had Julie and Ellen not worked through these issues, it could have greatly affected not only their relationship but the continuance of a wonderful ministry together.

Not Doing it Right

It didn't make much sense, but almost every time Ralph got a job, the same bad thing would happen. (The only exception was when he had a woman for a boss, and then everything went okay.) Ralph would be given certain responsibilities, often involving organization—which he was very good at. Yet inevitably, his boss would get angry with him for not doing things the "right" way. This was confusing for Ralph. He was actually getting in trouble for doing what he thought he was told to do. The catch was that often times the instructions had not been made clear. It also seemed as if his boss was just taking out frustration on Ralph and shifting blame on him though the fault was really his for not being more clear with his directions. Ralph enjoyed his work and was actually quite proficient at it. Yet this pattern seemed to keep occurring.

In prayer, we asked the Lord to show us when else Ralph may have felt this way. The Lord reminded him of a time when he was a boy and was given the responsibility of mowing the lawn. Though it was his first time, his father expected him to already know how to do it. So, despite the lack of instruction, he got out the mower and tried to start it up. He tried again and again, but nothing happened. He decided to ask his father for help. His father came out, checked the lawnmower, pulled the starter rope, and it immediately started. He made it look so easy! What was Ralph doing wrong?

The next time Ralph went to mow the lawn, the same thing happened. So once again Ralph had to ask his father for help. This repeated routine soon got to be annoying to his father who became very angry, so much so that he would no longer help Ralph start the mower. Not only that, he wouldn't let Ralph do anything else until he could start the mower by himself and then finish mowing the lawn. Ralph would pull and pull the starter rope until he was exhausted, frustrated and upset. Fortunately, a neighbor saw his plight and asked what was going on. Ralph explained his problem. After inspecting it, the neighbor showed Ralph that the sparkplug wire was disconnected. When it was hooked up, he could easily start the mower.

What Ralph realized was that when his father put the mower in the garage, he disconnected the sparkplug for safety's sake. He had done this assuming Ralph would know what to do. Every time Dad went to start the mower, he would reconnect the sparkplug and it would start. Unfortunately, Ralph never saw this part of the procedure because he always stood behind his father. So Ralph prayed, "Lord, I remember feeling very frustrated and hurt whenever I had to try and mow the lawn. I felt my father was very demanding and unfair. I couldn't start the mower no matter how hard I tried. He just expected me to somehow know that the sparkplug was disconnected. I did not deserve his anger or punishment. I choose to forgive him now. I also confess the resentment I have held towards him. I renounce my decision that, "No one will show me how; it is all up to me, and I will be blamed for not knowing what others were supposed to teach me."

Ralph was between jobs when he prayed through this memory. A few weeks later, a wonderful thing happened. He was hired for a new job where they paid him for the first two weeks of training. In this way, he would know exactly what was expected of him before he actually began to work. They also provided him with a handbook, which clearly laid out what his and other employees' responsibilities were. In addition, he was given a company phone list so if he had any questions about anything, he would know whom to contact. For the first time, Ralph was free to reap a job that didn't match his roots. He was free to succeed at what he really excelled in.

What do I Really Want to Do?

Dorothy came for a week of counseling because her boss had made the opportunity available. He had been so touched by the ministry he had received that he decided to pay all the expenses for any of his staff who wanted it as well. Though unaware of any pressing issues, Dorothy decided she would come anyway. As the ministry time got underway, it became apparent that Dorothy was not living the life God had intended for her—she wasn't living her passion. She was doing work that she was skilled at but it really wasn't an expression of who she was. And as a result, she was unhappy.

Previously, Dorothy had accepted a job which initially involved music, in which she had a degree. Soon after however, she got pulled into the office instead, because of pressing administration needs. Though she did excellent work and was very much appreciated, it wasn't what she really wanted to do. When asked what she really wanted to do, Dorothy shared about her love for music and her desire to teach. She wanted to live, not in the big city, but out in the country and teach children and adults to sing and play the piano. Yet, she felt guilty and selfish about pursuing these desires.

As Dorothy explored what it was like for her growing up, she shared many happy memories. She knew that her parents loved

Pray Through It

each other deeply in spite of the fact that her mother was rather "emotional", struggling from time to time with some internal issues which Dorothy's father was unable to "fix". Mom would sometimes complain and be short with Dad. As a little girl, Dorothy had seen her mother's emotional times as a source of conflict between her parents. And so she judged her mother and resolved not to express her own feelings and emotions, thus making the following decisions: "I won't be like Mother" and "I can't be spontaneous."

Now, realizing the connection between those decisions and what she was reaping in the present, Dorothy took her parents' relationship to the Lord in prayer. She told Him how her mother's emotionalism and the conflicts it had caused with her father had hurt her and how she had judged her mother resultantly. She confessed her sin and forgave her mother. She also renounced her decisions to not be like her mother and to not be spontaneous.

When Dorothy returned home she did something spontaneous! She pursued her passion. . . She quit her job and moved to the country. There she rented a small place and printed up some business cards which read: "Private Voice and Piano Lessons." She soon had some students and was on her way! She had finally found the freedom and ability to pursue her lifelong dream. One year later, her former boss shared that he had known all along that Dorothy didn't belong where she was (in his office). Yet he just couldn't let her go because she was such a wonderful worker. Despite his personal loss he is now very thankful for the healing that Dorothy received and the change that has transpired in her life.

Playing is Too Uncomfortable

As an adult, I came to recognize the importance of parents playing with their kids. Playing with your children is so meaningful to them, especially when you do something they like to do. It's funny though, even knowing that, I had no conscious recollection of wanting (or *not* wanting) my parents to play with me. It just seemed that when I was a kid adults really didn't play with little kids, though they might have with the older ones. Yet, as an adult I knew its importance and wanted to be the kind of dad that played with his kids.

I remember when my daughter was three I decided to make an all out effort to spend time playing with her. As I did, I noticed that it was very difficult for me to actually sit and play. I would find myself frequently getting up from playing to do something else. All kinds of other things would pop into my head to do just at the moment I'd get down on the floor with her, for instance, balance my checkbook (something that typically doesn't interest me at all!), vacuum the carpet for my wife, or make a phone call. At first, I wasn't aware of what I was doing. My actions seemed reasonable and even responsible. But one day it dawned on me and I knew I had some praying to do.

Why was the checkbook more important than playing with my daughter? Could it be that I was "fleeing"? Could it be that on some level playing with my daughter reminded my heart of times no one played with me? As I considered this, I saw it might be true. I saw that I probably was "fleeing" in order to avoid this uncomfortable feeling. If so, this impulse to flee was occurring despite the fact that I wasn't even aware of any specific hurtful memory. (It is amazing how we rarely or ever question our behavior and just assume that this is the way we are or that what we are doing is "normal.")

I shared with a friend what I had come to realize. Together we asked the Lord, if this were true, would He reveal any times when I wanted someone to play with me but no one did. As I waited, two different times came to mind. The first memory was of me as a toddler sitting on the beach. My mother was sitting in a lounge chair. I saw myself look over to her and then look away. The Lord indicated that, when I looked over at her, I wanted her to play with me, even though I didn't speak up. I realized that I had long ago given up thinking that she might play with me since she so rarely did. In another instance, I was on the floor and my mother had just given me Lincoln Logs to play with. Again, I wanted her to join me, but she didn't. Evidently she was too busy. These memories illustrated what I had felt so many times as a child. Yet in these two instances, I had clearly given up the idea that it could be any different.

I took these memories to the Lord in prayer. I shared the details of what happened and how I imagined it would have made me feel-- that I was alone and that others weren't interested in playing with me. I then forgave my mother, while confessing the judgment I had against her for not wanting to play with me. I also gave up my decision that I could not expect anyone to want to play with me.

Later on that day when I came home from work my daughter met me at the door and asked, "Daddy, do you want to play with me?" Just then my wife, not knowing what I had prayed through that day, asked, "So what happened today?" In reply, I pointed towards my daughter and said, "This!" Believe it or not, prior to that day, I don't ever remember my daughter asking me to play when I came home from work. Usually, I would have to initiate playing with her. But now the unspoken message emanating from my heart ("I can't expect anyone to play with me") was gone. Before this, my daughter probably wanted to play with me, but she sensed my negative decision and decided not to ask. Subsequently, I also found it easier to resist the temptation to "flee". In addition, playing with my daughter has become not only a very comfortable thing but also something I quite enjoy.

Abandonment Gone

Michelle was not doing well at all. She had experienced a breakdown a while back, and even after a year and half of counseling somewhere else, she was still feeling overwhelmed in doing even small tasks at work. She also told me that she felt she had no support systems in her life. As she shared, Michelle revealed she'd never felt bonded to her mother and had always felt like she was from a different family. She also shared with me the trauma of being molested by her father at age 4, along with a host of other hurtful memories.

After a while, I decided to have Michelle close her eyes and focus on the emotional pain she was feeling inside. As she did, she could feel the associated message in her heart of "nobody is there for me!" It became clear that the intense feeling of abandonment echoing from her past was at the center of her current emotional crisis.

I then asked Michelle if she would let Jesus come to the place where her pain was. When she said, "yes" she soon sensed Jesus' presence and heard Him tell her that she was special. She had really needed this, since she had come to believe in her heart that she was worthless and ugly because of the terrible things that had happened to her. To make matters worse, she had actually been told she was ugly. Just sharing about that was extremely painful. But when Jesus said to her, "No, My child, you are *precious*," she began to cry. Another painful lie lodged in her heart surfaced. She had decided that "nobody ever really wanted me!" Yet to this Jesus responded by saying, "*I* want you." As she got in touch with an even deeper layer of pain she cried out, "I'm abandoned!" Yet once again, Jesus gently responded by saying, "My daughter, I will *never* leave you or forsake you."

By speaking the truth to her heart, Jesus began displacing the lies that had been lodged there. In order to completely remove them, I encouraged her to pray through the times of hurt and pain she had shared that day. In prayer to Jesus, she shared her hurtful experiences and forgave her mother and father for the part they had played. She also confessed her judgments, her hatred, and her other sinful responses to the wounding she had received. Following this, I prayed a prayer which pronounced the forgiveness she had received. I then prayed for cleansing from all the defilement of the incredible abuse she had been through. All the while during this prayer she shook and cried.

Then a wonderful thing happened. She actually felt extreme pain of her past memories leave! In a relatively short time of prayer where about 20 major hurtful issues were covered (including molest, abandonment, verbal and physical abuse, alcoholism, and neglect) she was, by God's grace, able to forgive her father and mother. A week later, Michelle came back. There was a noticeable change in her. Her countenance was completely different. For the first time in a very long time she felt free. She had a genuine sense of well-being. The oppression she had been living under for years was gone!

Brad's Other Name

Brad came in for help for several reasons. Among them were struggles in his sexual relationship with his wife and depression. Early on in the counseling time it became apparent that another dynamic was occurring. Almost every time Brad would attempt to come to his appointments, something bad would happen. One time he had an onset of gout in his ankles. Another time, he slipped and broke his collar bone. On another occasion he twisted his ankle just before our session. He would often show up on crutches. Once, his car even caught on fire on the way to my office! Most of these things were beyond his control. It was as if some outside force was working against Brad every time he tried to get help. To say the least, these events were very discouraging. Yet, despite all this, Brad was determined to keep coming for counseling.

As he shared about what it was like growing up, it became clear that there's always been something working against him. When Brad was a boy, his father would often belittle him and put him down. He would call Brad all sorts of things containing the "f" word, almost as though the "f" word was Brad's other name. As you can imagine, it deeply wounded him. Often when Brad turned to his father for help, he got cursed instead. "You stupid %#@*&! Can't you do anything right?" There seemed to be a connection between Brad's being cursed by his father when he needed help and bad things happening to Brad when he sought help.

So we spent time together praying through as many incidents with the "f" word as Brad could remember. With each memory, we took the time for Brad to share what happened and how it made him feel. For each one, Brad also confessed any resentment he had towards his father and then forgave him. I prayed to break the power of the "f" word over him. Lastly, he renounced all the various ways he had come into agreement with the curses of his father.

This took several sessions to get through, but the time spent was well worth it. Brad's heart needed to receive healing for each and every time his father cursed him.

Then a wonderful change occurred. The phenomenon where something bad would happen to Brad whenever he sought help stopped. There were no longer any sore ankles or burnt cars to distract us from our work in prayer. Brad could now focus on the issues he had originally come to counseling for.

If You Get Angry, the Relationship is Over

At one time, Steve was afraid to show or share any angry feelings with friends because he felt it would mean the end of a relationship. As a result, he found it extremely difficult to share something when it involved irritation, misunderstanding or conflict. Instead, he would hide his true feelings and act as if everything was okay. Yet all the while, he'd feel his anger slowly turn to resentment, churning inside because it was not being expressed. When he eventually did share, he would overreact because so much had built up over time. Then he would just feel stupid.

Steve decided to take this issue to prayer and asked the Lord, "When in Steve's past did he feel that sharing his anger would result in the end of a friendship?" The Lord reminded him of his parents' divorce, when he was a little boy. He had often seen his parents arguing and witnessed how neither one ever really felt heard. He also noted how nothing ever seemed to get resolved, either. He remembered feeling his mother's pain, but at the same time watched how she chose to bottle it all up inside. He also saw his father's hurt. When they finally divorced, Steve concluded that it was the result of so much anger and fighting.

Steve then prayed, "Lord, I remember my father and mother arguing when I was little. It was very scary for me, and what's worse, it resulted in them divorcing. I really wanted them to work things out. But instead, I believed the lie that anger will bring about the end of a relationship. I forgive them for not hearing each other, for not working things out and for divorcing. I give up my decision that if I share my anger it will mean the end of a relationship."

Subsequently, Steve reported finding that the anxiety he felt around sharing angry feelings subsided. He also found himself over-reacting less when he legitimately needed to share anger. By dealing with his bitter roots, Steve was able to reach a new level of maturity and closeness in his relationships with others.

Should I Grieve?

Joe and Peggy wanted so much to have a child. Unfortunately, they went through the difficult experience of miscarriage. After losing the baby, Peggy went through a time of grieving. Joe, however, was troubled because he didn't. He was disappointed, naturally, but he never really experienced any crying or sadness over the loss of his child. When Joe asked the doctor if anything was wrong with him, the doctor told him that, since he had never actually seen the baby whereas Peggy had carried it in her womb, it only made sense that he wouldn't have any attachment to the child. Therefore, there was really nothing to grieve. In addition, Joe was told that what he was experiencing was "normal" for most men. Despite this explanation, Joe was still troubled by his lack of grief.

Joe identified his inability to grieve over the loss of his child as bad fruit. He found it hard to accept that this was "normal" for men. So in prayer we asked the Lord to show him other times when he was unable to grieve. He remembered as a child having a dog. We asked the Lord what this memory had to do with not being able to grieve. Joe remembered how he came home one day to find the family dog was gone. When he asked what had happened, he was told that it got hit by a car. His father had found the dog's body and put it in the trash. His dad later went out and got another dog to replace it. There was no discussion about the matter. No one cried. No one openly grieved their obvious loss. Joe got the message that "life goes on—deal with it!"

For homework after our session together, Joe was given an assignment to write out what he missed about his dog, what its name was, why he liked him, what they did together, etc. As he was writing, Joe remembered how his dog had been so faithful to him, greeting him every time he came home from school, where no one else in his family ever did. He remembered just hanging out with his dog when he felt alone and misunderstood. His dog was there for him and always loved him. When Joe shared these things sadness began to come over him. At first he thought this was rather absurd. When I asked, "Why?" he replied, "He was just a dog." "Yes. But you loved him," I said. I then encouraged Joe to say out loud, "I miss my dog." And as he did the tears began to flow. He was finally able to feel the love for this dog that he had missed so very much, love that he had stuffed way down deep inside all these years. Now, with his heart free to grieve (free to be normal), anger came up as well, towards his father—one, for not letting him see the dog after he had died, and two, for not letting Joe bury him.

In prayer, Joe said, "Heavenly Father, I bring before you the incident of the death of my dog. I now realize that it really hurt me when my father threw him in the trash and didn't even give me a chance to say "Good-bye." It made my dog seem worthless, like a piece of trash, something to be discarded. I needed my parents to help me grieve. Because they didn't, it made me feel that grief is somehow wrong, bad, and scary. I wrongly decided it wasn't worth crying about. I also believed the lie that my feelings don't matter. I confess my bitterness towards my father, and I choose to forgive him for what he did. I renounce my decisions that "my feelings don't matter" and "It's not worth crying about."

After praying, more sadness began to well up in Joe. This sadness was about the child his wife had miscarried. Joe was now free to feel his grief—grief that was no longer suppressed by his negative heart-felt decisions. He began to feel how much he really had been looking forward to meeting his child, to holding him, and fathering him. It took a little time, but Joe was able to work through the process of grieving the loss of his baby. Joe was also free to do the same in other areas of his life. This experience brought another blessing; it drew Joe and Peggy closer together. Having finally shared in one another's grief they felt more united in facing the future together.

I Can't Go Any Faster

Fran worked in the bakery department at a local grocery store. Over a period of time, Fran's boss had made it clear that she needed to learn to work faster. However, she couldn't do so without sacrificing the quality of her work. This was very frustrating for her, and she found herself saying, "The harder I try, the slower I go." Fran was familiar with the process of identifying bad fruit with regard to the principle of sowing and reaping. So, as she thought about this phenomenon in her life, she came to recognize it as "bad fruit". She then asked the Lord to reveal the root of it.

About four weeks later, the Lord brought to Fran's mind a memory of her sixth birthday. Her parents had asked her what she wanted that year, and she told them her dream was to be on a television program which featured a big birthday party each week. For this special party, some children were selected to join the host on the show for a spectacular celebration complete with cake, balloons and confetti! Much to Fran's surprise, one day her parents told her that *she* had actually been chosen to be on that show! When the big day came, her parents took her to the studio. However, upon arriving, she quickly learned that her dream celebration wasn't going to be what she thought. The sets weren't real-- they were just props. Every move, every word, was scripted. And she was told exactly where to go and when, how to smile and how to sit. . .

Finally, the time came for the children to march through the "birthday door" and sit down at the "birthday table"! Despite her initial disappointment, Fran tried to make the best of things, especially when she was given a Popsicle and some cake! Yet no sooner was she seated at the table with the goodies, than she was whisked off again, sent back stage and told to go sit with her parents. Just like that, the moment was gone... The dream was over... And worse yet, she realized that she had left her Popsicle on stage, melting under the bright camera lights! Needless to say, in all the hurry of getting the show filmed, Fran's joy was stolen. This left her wishing she had been given time to *slow down* and enjoy it all. This little girl, out of the tremendous hurt and disappointment she felt, made a decision-- "I am *never* going to hurry again!"

As an adult, Fran was able to make the connection between what had happened so many years ago and what was occurring on her job in the present. With this understanding, she prayed through her disappointing birthday experience, pouring out her hurt feelings and sadness to the Lord. She forgave the people who had let her down. And lastly, she gave up her decision to "never hurry again".

After praying, Fran felt a wall come down within her heart and she could feel her inner resistance to hurrying start to fade. Very soon after that, she found she was able to work quite a bit faster while not compromising the quality of what she did!

Bearing Good Fruit

Let us not become weary in doing good,
for at the proper time we will reap a harvest
if we do not give up.
Galatians 6:9

God knows there is good fruit coming, so don't give up!
Although the focus of this book has been on how to deal with
troubles, in closing I'd like to lay those thoughts aside and leave you
with a word of encouragement... *Live life!* Life begins and
continues in your relationship with God and Him alone. Continue
sowing good that you may reap good, not only to reap in this life but
also in eternity. Find your purpose in life *in Him*, and live it! Don't
drift from it by focusing all your attention on the search for bitter
roots. Enjoy the good things the Lord has given you and done for
you. *Enjoy Him.* Focus on what is wonderful around you, and let
Him know how thankful you are. Don't let the bad fruit that hasn't
yet been uprooted distract you from *enjoying the Lord today.* Make
a conscious choice to embrace
life, to spend time with those
you love, and to live in the
present. Please don't get
hung up on figuring out every
little trouble and issue from
your past. If the Lord hasn't
yet revealed or dealt with it,

Don't let the bad fruit that hasn't
yet been uprooted distract you
from enjoying the Lord today.

then He has a reason, a wonderful reason, with you in mind. If He
isn't anxious about it, then why should you be? Yes, we can be
mindful but not anxious, diligent but patient as well. If you identify
something as bad fruit, examine it and pray about it. But if you
find no identifiable root issues, then go on with your day!

There are people out there to be encouraged and loved, and there
is our Lord to be worshipped and adored. If we are abiding in Jesus,
then what you and I have to offer at any moment is sufficient for
what He is doing in and through us. He will get to our "stuff" in
good time. He knows our beginnings, our endings and everything in
between. We need to learn to rest in His peace and to feel His

heartbeat within us. We need to spend time with Him. Let's trust Him with our past, present and future, for life is an incredible journey when you're riding with the One who knows you best!

Now He who supplies seed to the sower and bread for food will supply and multiply your seed for sowing and increase the harvest of your righteousness; you will be enriched in everything for all liberality, which through us is producing thanksgiving to God.
2 Corinthians 9:10-11 (NASB)

May the Lord increase your harvest of the good fruit of righteousness as you seek Him in all things, apply His provision when praying through root issues, and continue sowing good – to Him be the glory!

 # Miscellaneous Questions

What if a memory comes to mind that I have already prayed through before?

Ask the Lord what else He is trying to show you. Often the Lord does this because there is some other aspect concerning that particular issue which needs to be prayed through. Each time, perhaps, a different judgment or lie we believed is being revealed. Possibly, we were unable to see these other things before because we weren't ready. Sometimes, we would not have been able to recognize them until He had worked through something else in our life first.

What if, after praying through some memories, nothing has changed?

This could be for several reasons. Sometimes, the good fruit doesn't come right away. Some things are the result of our sin and, therefore, what was set in motion will need to be dealt with over a period of time. Divorce is an example of this. Though future reaping may have been stopped through confession, certain consequences have already been set in motion which will need to be walked through. Sometimes, there are more memories along the same theme which need to be prayed through as well.

What if I feel worse after praying through something?

This can occur in some instances. This is usually because many of the issues we have avoided are now surfacing. If we have been kept from grieving, there will be a lot of catching up to do. If we have not allowed ourselves to feel sadness or to cry, there is a backlog of issues to be processed. Just embrace it, trust the Lord in the process, and know that eventually you will get to the other side.

How do I get others to deal with their root issues when their bad fruit is so plain to me?

The best way is to deal with your *own* bad fruit first. This will accomplish a number of things. First of all, it will produce good fruit that hopefully the other person will see without you telling them. Also, your root issues will no longer be a stumbling block for them, which had in the past caused them to react and shift blame on to you. As a result, they may really start to notice a change in you which may cause them to start noticing the bad fruit in their lives, knowing that you are no longer the problem. In addition, by praying through your issues, you have something to share with them—about your bad fruit, your root issues, how you prayed and what changed. Let your life and your testimony do the work. Let the light of what Jesus has done in your life shine!

Do I always have to be with someone else when I identify and pray through my issues?

There are times when the Lord will bring up something when you are alone with Him. Go ahead and pray through it, while it is fresh on your heart. But, I would still encourage you to share what you had prayed through and what happened with someone else at a later date, asking them to pray for you as well (James 5:16).

I'm just like you. Though I help others using the gifts and abilities God has given and developed in me, I need other people with their gifting and love to help me work through my issues. I need them to reassure me. I, too, experience times of not being able to clarify bad fruit and identify root issues on my own. God wants us to minister to one another. He promises a blessing when we do. So, in answer to your question, no, it's not necessary, but it's definitely recommended—not only by me, but especially by the Lord.

What if the person I resented, who hurt me, doesn't think that they hurt me or that they did anything wrong? What if they think I am wrong about how I perceived the situation?

The wonderful thing about praying through root issues is that others don't have to admit it for us to be set free. In addition, what really matters is not so much how others perceived what happened but how *we* perceived it. We bear bad fruit for what *we* judged and resented, whether or not we had the details or perspective on the situation right.

Some of us have resented people for doing the right thing. Often, this is because we have a history of expecting to be treated a certain way. So, we respond or react from this bitter-root expectation. Some people have even resented God-- and we know *He* doesn't do anything wrong. Regardless, if we responded in a sinful manner and didn't deal with it, then we have sown something bad and are bound to reap from it. We need to pray through it.

Why doesn't God reveal and deal with all my unresolved issues? Why does He take so much time to do it?

There are a number of reasons for this. Sometimes, the Lord is training us, teaching us to see that He loves us, even if we are not perfect. Some of us need to know that we are still loved even when we are struggling with sin. Sometimes, the Lord is trying to bring out some hidden trait in us that we never knew existed, and He knows the present situation will eventually bring forth. Sometimes, He wants to teach us about the power of *overcoming.* He allows certain things to remain, so that as we struggle, we grow and mature in spite of them. Besides, we gain authority in what we overcome. He allows this to build character and to establish a firm relationship with Him, which is so much more important than anything else. Sometimes, one certain issue needs to be healed first, before moving on to the next issue. We often need time between trials to walk out (and grow accustomed to) the change He has done in us.

In some cases, there are lessons that can be learned only through suffering. Jesus never promised a life free from suffering but rather that He would be there when we go through it. There are times when we are called to suffer for Christ, for His reputation. This may involve fighting for our marriages, but not for ourselves. To lay down my life for another is an act of love, doing whatever it takes to change me and become the person God wants me to be so that I can help another. I may need to battle against selfishness, bitterness, revenge. I may need to stick it out in a difficult job situation, a relationship with someone who has betrayed me, an unfulfilling or tough marriage, or hard financial times.

Keep in mind that sometimes the reasons why God doesn't immediately deal with our unresolved issues are unique to the circumstances and seasons in our lives. Some things will not be revealed until a certain season is complete. Yet most often, He just wants us to learn to seek Him with all our hearts, and to trust Him for the reasons.

What about 2 Corinthians 5:17: "Therefore, if anyone is in Christ, he is a new creature; the old has passed away; behold, the new has come"? (NASB)

When you read the context of this verse, the "old" is the way we tried to live without God and His provision. The "new" that has come through Christ, is our relationship with God which allows us to reconcile those things in our lives that stand between us and Him. In 2 Corinthians 5:20, we are charged to be reconciled to God. This passage is directed at believers, not unbelievers. Being reconciled to God is something *we* must do. Confessing our sins and forgiving others is one of those ways. And praying through root issues is one of the areas where we put this into practice.

Appendix A – Feeling Words

Though there are lots of other words to describe how one feels, the words listed below are those often used in describing "hurt"-- when one was hurt by another person or a circumstance. Don't limit yourself to these-- they are merely a good place to start. Use this list when trying to describe how you felt when you were hurt, especially when praying through past root issues.

Descriptive Feeling Words of Hurt

cold	laughed at	stupid
compared	lied to	suffocated
condemned	like a ...	taken advantage of
controlled	like a failure	tormented
crazy	like a jerk	torn
crippled	like an idiot	trampled upon
criticized	looked down upon	trapped
crushed	lost	unappreciated
cursed	made fun of	unclean
damaged	maimed	uncovered
dead	manipulated	unjustly treated
debased	mislead	unloved
deceived	mistreated	unsafe
defiled	mocked	unsure
deprived	naked	unwanted
destroyed	needy	unwelcome
dirty	neglected	unworthy
discouraged	not needed	used
disgraced	nothing	violated
doomed	numb	vulnerable
dreadful	obligated	wasted
dumb	offended	weighted down
embarrassed	oppressed	weird
empty inside	out of control	worn out
exposed	out of my mind	worse
falsely accused	overcome	worthless
foolish	overpowered	wounded
forgotten	overwhelmed	wrong
ganged-up on	plotted against	wronged
harassed	powerless	

Appendix A – Feeling Words (continued)

General Feeling Words of Hurt

afflicted	confounded	frightened	mad
afraid	confused	frustrated	mean
agitated	depressed	furious	miserable
alone	despair	greedy	pained
angry	disappointed	grieved	rejected
anguished	dishonored	guilty	sad
anxious	embarrassed	hated	terrible
awful	empathetic	hurt	terrified
bad	envious	ignored	weak
betrayed	exasperated	injured	
bitter	fearful	lonely	

General Words Describing Change

The following is a list of feeling words often used when describing how one might feel after they have prayed through something, especially when there has been a sense or experience of change.

a sense of worth	found	released
alive	free	relieved
at rest	good	renewed
better	grateful	rested
big inside	great	restored
blessed	happy	safe
clean	healed	seen
clear headed	heard	strengthened
clothed	hopeful	ten feet tall
comforted	joy	thankful
confident	light	touched
content	lighter	understood
courage	loved	uplifted
covered	myself again	wanted
defended	new	wanted
delighted	no longer...	warm
empowered	not as ...	whole
encouraged	peace	wonderful
filled	quiet inside	young again
forgiven	radiant	